THE WHIT

Readings and Prayers in Honor of the Seven
Sorrows of the Blessed Virgin Mary

Father Peter O. Akpoghiran, J.C.D.

The White Lily of Heaven: Readings and Prayers in Honor of the Seven Sorrows of the Blessed Virgin Mary © 2018 Copyright Peter O. Akpoghiran, J.C.D.
Publisher: Transfiguration Press, New Orleans, Louisiana, USA
Email: director@transfigurationpress.com
Printed in the United States of America.

ISBN-13: 978-1547283934

ISBN-10: 1547283939

Nihil Obstat:	Reverend Vinh D. Luu, J.C.L.
	Judge, Metropolitan Tribunal of the
	Archdiocese of New Orleans, Louisiana
	August 6, 2018
	Feast of the Transfiguration of the Lord
Imprimatur:	Most Reverend Gregory M. Aymond
	Archbishop of New Orleans
	August 15, 2018
	Solemnity of the Assumption of the Blessed Virgin Mary

The *Nihil Obstat* and *Imprimatur* are official declarations that a book or a pamphlet is free of doctrinal error. No implication is contained therein that those who have granted the Nihil Obstat and Imprimatur agree with the contents, opinions, or statements expressed.

TABLE OF CONTENT

WEEK 2: THE SECOND SORROW OF THE BLESSED VIRGIN MARY - THE FLIGHT TO EGYPT 26

INTRODUCTION

The knowledge of the sorrows of the Blessed Virgin Mary is fundamental to a deeper appreciation of the important role she played in the redemption wrought for us by her Son, Jesus Christ. The Blessed Virgin Mary merits our gratitude for the many sorrows she suffered in union with her Son, Jesus Christ. We can show our gratitude by meditating upon her sorrows, by showing our compassion to her, and by praying to her in her capacity and advocacy as the Mother of Sorrows, or in Latin: *Mater Dolorosa*. The sorrows she suffered on earth are innumerable. However, with the passage of time, devotion to the seven of her sorrows became popular. The founders of the Order of the Servants of Mary (the Servite Order) often meditated upon her sorrows. Thus, beginning from the thirteen century, the friars of the Servite Order began to promote devotions to the sorrows of Mary, especially her seven principal sorrows. The devotion to the seven sorrows of Mary has continued to this day.

The purpose of this book is to aid people to further develop a greater devotion to the Blessed Virgin Mary, especially in her title and advocacy as the Mother of Sorrows. Those who read and meditate on the sorrows of the Blessed Virgin Mary and who have a prayerful devotion to her seven principal sorrows have been assured by Our Lord and by Our Lady of numerous graces and promises. Thus, you will also find in this book the promises of Our Lord and of Our Lady to those who are devoted to the Blessed Virgin Mary under her title and advocacy as Our Lady of Sorrows or as Mother of Sorrows.

Another purpose of this book is also to provide study materials for meditation on the seven sorrows of the Blessed Virgin Mary and to help people better appreciate the roles she played in the redemptive mission of Jesus Christ.

The main sources for this book are the Holy Bible, the *Mystical City of God* by Venerable Mary of Agreda, and *The Life of the Blessed Virgin Mary* and *The Dolorous Passion of Our Lord Jesus Christ* – both written by Catherine Emmerich. All these and other sources used in this book have the imprimaturs of the competent ecclesiastical authority. This book itself also has ecclesiastical approval.

This book is divided into seven weeks. Each week is devoted to one of the seven sorrows of the Blessed Virgin Mary. Each week is divided into seven days, and each day is divided into two parts. The first part of each day is devoted to the events surrounding the life and sorrow of the Blessed Virgin Mary under study for the week. The second part of each day of the week is a prayer to or in honor of Our Lady of Sorrows. The seventh day of each week is devoted to reflections on some of the themes of the preceding six days. The meditations of the seventh day of each week help to sum up the themes of the week.

The 7 weeks in this book have been numbered Day 1 to Day 49. Thus, this book is also intended to serve as a 7-week or a 49-day do-it-yourself retreat with the Blessed Virgin Mary as we share with her in her many sorrows and sufferings and as we offer her our spiritual consolations, companionship, and compassion.

Thus, the arrangement of the study materials and prayers in this book is such that each week is dedicated to one of the seven sorrows of the Blessed Virgin. In this way, a careful and methodological study, meditation, and prayer regarding the seven sorrows of the Blessed Virgin Mary can be done within a period of seven weeks.

This book serves a triple-purpose, namely: to narrate events surrounding the seven principal sorrows of the Blessed Virgin Mary, to offer meditations and reflections on the dolors of the Blessed Virgin Mary, and to provide prayers to and in honor of Mary, Mother of Sorrows.

There is a certain order to the arrangement of the prayers in this book. The first day of each week is a prayer of reparation to the Mother of Sorrows; the second day of each week is a prayer of consolation and compassion to the Mother of Sorrows; and the third day of each week is an intercessory prayer to Our Blessed Mother of Sorrows for a specific, determinate intention, such as prayer for priests, prayer for religious, prayer for married people, prayer for single people, etc. The fourth day of each week is a special intention prayer to the Sorrowful Mother. The fifth day of

each week is a prayer of compassion and com-
memoration in honor of the 7 sorrows of Our Lady.

There were also innumerable occasions of joys
during the earthy sojourn of the Blessed Mother
and many occasions of heavenly joys for her more
so now that she is in heaven. Thus, each sixth day
of the week in this book is dedicated to prayers in
honor of the several earthly and heavenly joys of
Mary. And the seventh day of each week is a
prayer of praise in honor of Our Lady. The prayers
on the seventh day of the seventh week, however,
are prayers of consecration to the Mother of Sorrows. Thus, the 49-day spiritual program, journey,
and retreat with our Most Sorrowful and Blessed
Mother culminate in an act of consecration to the
Mother of Sorrows.

One may begin the 49-day or 7-week do-it-
yourself spiritual retreat provided in this book on
any day of the month and on any month of the
year. One may also commence it 49 days prior to a
forthcoming Marian liturgical feast. In this way,
the 49th or last day of this personal retreat would
end on the said Marian feastday with the prayer of
consecration to the Mother of Sorrows. The consecration may be renewed annually or on September
15, the feast of Our Lady of Sorrows. The events
narrated in this book, as well its reflections and
prayers are sources of meditation, spiritual read-
ing, and graces. The mysteries of her sorrows and
sufferings are so vast and profound that one gains

further insights and more abundant merits each time one studies and meditates on them anew.

Notwithstanding the systematic arrangement of the narratives, meditations, and prayers in this book, any of the narratives, meditations, and prayers in this book can be said, read, recited, or prayed on any day of the year. This can happen, for example, when you have been divinely inspired to do so or when a particular narrative, meditation, or prayer in this book speaks to a special intention or to a particular situation of yours.

All praise and glory be to God for his graces, protections, blessings, and mercies in my life. Many thanks to Archbishop Gregory M. Aymond, Archbishop of New Orleans, U.S.A. and to Bishop John O. Afareha, Bishop of Warri Diocese, Nigeria, for their support. I am also grateful to Father Vinh D. Luu, J.C.L., for his reviews and comments regarding this book.

May this book serve as a sacramental to draw you closer to God and God closer to you. May the Most High continue to bless you with his powerful right hand. May he raise you up and show you the light of his divine countenance. May the blessings and protection of the Blessed Virgin Mary, Mother of Sorrows, be with you now and forever. Amen.

Rev. Fr. Peter O. Akpoghiran, J.C.D.
September 15, 2018
Feast of Our Lady of Sorrows.

WEEK 1: THE FIRST SORROW OF THE BLESSED VIRGIN MARY - THE PROPHESY OF SIMEON

Simeon blessed them and said to Mary his mother, "Behold, this child is destined for the fall and the rise of many in Israel, and to be a sign that will be opposed — and a sword shall pierce your heart — so that the thoughts of many hearts may be revealed." (Lk. 2:34-35).

Day 1:   **The Old Testament Law on the Presentation of the First Born to the Lord**

1. Opening Prayer

O Most Holy and Righteous Father, in union with the love of your well-beloved Son, I commend this spiritual retreat of mine to you in honor of the sorrows of the Blessed Virgin Mary. Bless me so that I may praise your holy name, enlighten my understanding so that I may see the wonders of your word, and strengthen my will so that I may worthily, attentively, and devoutly commence and complete this spiritual journey with the Blessed Virgin Mary in honor of her sorrows, and so deserve to be richly blessed by your Divine Majesty. O Most Loving Lord Jesus, in union with the divine intention and love with which you gave praise to God the Father while on earth, I offer this holy journey to you. O Most Compassionate Holy Spirit, in union with the merits of the precious

Blood of Jesus, I also offer you this spiritual journey of faith. I humbly beseech you to purify, strengthen, and guard my intellect, will, and heart now and forever. Amen.

V. Sorrowful and Immaculate Heart of Mary.

R. Pray for us who have recourse to you.

Let us pray. Direct, we beseech you, O Lord, all our actions by your holy inspiration, carry them on by your gracious assistance, that every word and work of ours may always begin from you and by you be happily ended. Through Christ our Lord. Amen.

2. The Law of the Presentation of the First Born in the Old Testament

According to the Law of Moses, a woman who gives birth to a son should not touch anything sacred or enter the temple until forty days after the birth of the son. At the end of the forty days she was to offer a year-old lamb as a burnt offering and a turtledove or young pigeon as purification for sin before she could be re-admitted to the temple. The woman who could not afford a lamb offered instead two turtledoves or two young pigeons. (Lv. 12:2–8; 22:4). The Lord also commanded that any child or any animal that first opens the womb belongs to the Lord; therefore, every firstborn, whether of human being or of beast, shall be consecrated to the Lord. (Ex. 13:1-2, 12). With regard to first born sons among the Israelites, the consecration of the first born son was established so that the parents of any first born son might hope that their first born son would be the promised Messiah.

3. Act of Reparation to the Sorrowful and Immaculate Heart of Mary

O Blessed Virgin Mary, Mother of Sorrows, I present you the Sacred Heart of Jesus, your Son, which abounds in all beatitude. O most tender Mother, look upon the Sacred Heart of Jesus, overflowing with ineffable blessedness, and accept this prayer as an act of reparation from me to you. See in the Sacred Heart of Jesus all the divine love whereby from all eternity he freely chose you to be his Mother; he freely preserved you from all taint of original sin, and he freely adorned you with all graces and all virtues. See therein all the tenderness with which you cherished him; all the constant unfailing love with which, during the whole time of his sojourn on earth, he, the King of the Universe, obeyed you as a son his mother; and especially in the hour of his death, when, as though forgetting his own intolerable anguish, and touched to the heart by your desolation, he provided for you a guardian and a son. See therein that love beyond comprehension with which he showed you how precious you are in his sight, when on the day of your most joyous Assumption he exalted you high above all the choirs of angels and the saints, and crowned you Queen of Heaven and Earth. And, O most loving Mother, be to me a loving and protective Mother, and my compassionate advocate both in life and in death. Amen.

V. Mother of love, of sorrow, and of mercy.

R. Pray for us who have recourse to you.

Let us pray. O God and Father of our Lord Jesus Christ, a festive day for heaven and earth was it when the Blessed Virgin Mary took the baby Jesus to the Temple and offered him to you. He is the Living Bread, the Treasure of your Divinity. Rich, O my Lord and God, was the oblation, and you poured forth, in return, many blessings to Mary and to the rest of the human race. Pardon us sinners who have turned from the straight path, console the afflicted, help the needy, enrich the poor, succor the weak, and enlighten the ignorant. I praise you for your merciful condescension toward Mary in choosing her as the Mother of your only-begotten Son and our Lord Jesus Christ. Who lives and reigns with you and the Holy Spirit, one God, forever and ever. Amen.

Day 2: The Reason for the Presentation of Jesus in the Temple

1. The Reason Why Mary and Joseph Presented the Child Jesus in the Temple

Mary knew she did not need to fulfill the law which required her ritual purification because she is exempt from the stain of original sin and because she is pure in body and soul. She also knew that Jesus was conceived by the power of the Holy Spirit and that she is a virgin. She also knew she brought forth the Savior of the world without the pains of child-bearing. Nonetheless, she did not hesitate to humble herself to fulfill the Law of Moses; for she desired not to do her own will, but the will of the Lord. She also knew that Jesus, as God, did not need to be consecrated to God; however, she obligated herself to observe the requirements of the Mosaic law for the sake of righteousness.

Furthermore, it was the will of the Most Holy Trinity that God the Son should be taken to the temple and consecrated to God the Father as stipulated in the law of the old dispensation. This divine will was known to Mary, the Mother of life and of the Incarnate Word. Mary and Joseph also already knew that Jesus is the promised Messiah; nonetheless, they took Jesus to the temple to consecrate him to God the Father in order to fulfill the will of the Most Blessed Trinity and the requirement of the Mosaic Law.

2. Act of Consolation and Compassion to the Mother of Sorrows

O most loving Mother of our Lord Jesus Christ, I congratulate you and rejoice with you on the occasion of the presentation of our Lord Jesus Christ in the temple at Jerusalem. I beseech you, by the love which caused him to take flesh in the bosom of your most pure virginal womb, that you would supply for my defects in his service and yours. O most benign Mother, who is ever ready to assist me with maternal tenderness in all my necessities, I offer you the superabundant beatitude of the Sacred Heart of Jesus, who chose you from all eternity, before all creatures, to be his Mother. O Queen of Heaven and Earth who is exalted above all the choirs of angels and all creatures, you are my advocate; preserve and protect me this day and every day of my life from all mortal and venial sins. O Blessed Mother of Sorrows, I invoke and call upon you. By your intercession, may my soul be filled with the treasures and mercies of God. Bless me with your favors and protection in this life, and afterwards with eternal life. Incline your merciful eyes to your child here who devoutly invokes you and obtain for me the assistance of your maternal tenderness, the forgiveness of my sins, the favor of your presence and protection at the hour of my death, and the fruit of eternal salvation. Amen.

Say 3 Hail Marys.

Let us pray. O Blessed Trinity, who has neither commencement nor termination, who abounds ever in joy and beatitude, and who imparts eternal glory and blessedness to the angels and saints, I give you thanks for the Virgin Mary, the White Lily of Heaven, who is blessed above all creatures. I extol with the highest gratitude the incomprehensible omnipotence, the inscrutable wisdom, and the ineffable goodness of the Ever-Blessed Trinity. I beseech all the celestial choirs of angels and all the saints to praise you, on my behalf, for all the blessings and privileges you have bestowed upon her. Through Christ our Lord. Amen.

Day 3: The Presentation of the Lord in the Temple

1. The Procession to the Temple

The ritual purification of a woman who gave birth to a son and the presentation of her newly born son both take place forty days after the birth of her son. Thus, on the morning of the day of her ritual purification and the presentation of the Lord in the temple, Mary and Joseph took the Child Jesus, wrapped in swaddling clothes, to the temple. Mary carried him on her arms. They had with them a pair of turtle-doves.[1]

The Holy Family was joined by the guardian angels of Mary and by tens of thousands of angels who descended from heaven for this occasion. These angels formed guards of honor around the Holy Family, and they all with the Holy Family processed from Bethlehem to the temple in Jerusalem. They angels were visible to the members of the Holy Family only. Some of the angels sang

---

[1] Lev. 12:1-4; Lk. 2:24.

hymns of the sweetest and most enchanting harmony in honor of their Infant God, which were heard also by members of the Holy Family only.

Having arrived at the temple-gate, the most Blessed Mother was filled with new and exalted sentiments of joy. Joining the other women in the temple, she bowed and knelt to adore the Lord in spirit and in truth in his holy temple and she presented herself before the exalted Majesty of God with his Son on her arms. Mary and Joseph were filled with divine joy and light and with new blessings by the Holy Spirit.

2. Intercessory Prayer to Our Lady of Sorrows for Priests and Religious

Prayer for Priests: O Blessed ever-Virgin Mary, Mother of Sorrows, your Divine Son, our Lord Jesus Christ, came from heaven upon this earth in order to be the light of the world, to rescue it from the darkness of sin, to seek and know his sheep as a good Shepherd, to give us spiritual nourishment and eternal life, to teach us the way of heaven, and to open its gates, which had been closed by our sins. I join with you in thanking your Son and our Lord Jesus Christ for instituting the sacrament of holy orders so that, through our priests, his Body and Blood and the other sacraments would be administered to us. I also join with you in praying for our Catholic priests so that, marked by a special degree of holiness and placed under your maternal care and protection, they may continue to grow in holiness and grace and to win more souls for Christ. Amen.

I pray also for all those priests who are devoted to you, those who are known to me, and those who have asked for my prayers. Bring them closer to your Immaculate Heart and to the Divine Light. O Mother of priests, may your wonders, protection, and blessings be more openly revealed to them. Through your intercession, may there be more efficient and worthy ministers of Jesus Christ. He lives and reigns with the Father and the Holy Spirit, one God, forever and ever. Amen.

Mother of Jesus our Eternal Priest, pray for us.

Mary, Mother and Queen of the clergy, pray for us.

Mother Mary, Queen of the Priestly Heart of Jesus, pray for us.

Prayer for Members of Institutes of Consecrated Life and Societies of Apostolic Life. O Blessed Virgin Mary, Mother of the consecrated, I give joyful thanks and praise to Jesus Christ, who, from the immense abundance of his mercies and favors, has called and chosen his faithful to follow him as members of institutes of consecrated life and societies of apostolic life. By the efficacy of your intercession and your protection, may they follow him faithfully and persevere in their vocation and in the service of God. Shield all the members of the consecrated eremitical life, the order of virgins, the religious institutes, the secular institutes, and the societies of apostolic life from any and all dangers to their eternal salvation and to their persons. Attend, O Mother most gracious, to their material and spiritual needs and provide for them. By your guidance and protection, may they take only those decisions and actions that are for the greater glory and exultation of the holy name of God and for the salvation of their soul. I humbly implore you to direct and guide them, to defend and protect them, and to bring them to eternal glory. May Jesus Christ, in his divine providence, take good care of them, govern them according to his most holy will, draw them closer to his Sacred Heart, and, when their labors on earth are over, reward them with heavenly inheritance and recompense forever and ever. Amen.

Say 3 Hail Marys.

Let us pray. O Most Loving Lord Jesus Christ, by your pierced Heart, pierce the hearts of our clergy and members of institutes of consecrated life and societies of apostolic life with the arrow of your love so that they may be holy and so that they may be entirely filled with the strength of your Divinity and so please you always. Amen.

Day 4:   The Prophesy of Simeon

1. Simeon the Prophet and Anna the Prophetess

Now there was a man in Jerusalem whose name was Simeon. This man was righteous and devout, awaiting the consolation of Israel, and the Holy Spirit was upon him. It had been revealed to him by the Holy Spirit that he would not see death before he had seen the Messiah of the Lord. (Lk. 2:25-26). This holy, high-priest Simeon, moved by the Holy Spirit, entered the temple at that time (Lk. 2:27). He went to where Mary stood with the Infant Jesus in her arms. He saw Jesus, Mary, and Joseph enveloped in the shining light and glory of God.

The prophetess Anna had also come to the temple at the same hour. She, too, approached Mary, the Infant Jesus, and Joseph; she also saw them surrounded by the wonderful light of heaven. Anna was eighty-four years old; she had lived seven years with her husband after her marriage, and thereafter as a widow. She never left the temple, where she worshiped God night and day with fasting and prayer. (Lk. 2:36-37).

11

2. Special Intention Prayer to the Mother of Sorrows

O Blessed Virgin Mary, Mother of Sorrows, you are the ornament and beauty of the human race. You are the wonder of God's omnipotence, the exact copy of the perfections of Christ, the reflection of all his actions, and the mirror of the works of the Holy Spirit. You united yourself entirely to the One to whom you gave human form in your most sacred womb. You are a worthy Teacher of the Church militant, the sweet relief of the Church suffering, and the special joy of the Church triumphant. Let all the nations know your virtues and greatness, and let all ages praise and bless you.

May our Divine Maker be eternally blessed and magnified! You are most blessed among women, distinguished and chosen among all creatures! Let all generations congratulate, know, and praise you! May you enjoy for all eternity the excellence given to you by your Divine Son and our God! May Jesus, looking upon you, have mercy on me. If I should grieve him, plead my cause before him and obtain for me the pardon for my sins. We do not wonder that he should favor us so much, since you are his Mother and our Mother and Queen. Obtain for us his mercies and the effects of his redemption. O ever-Virgin Mary, whose heart a sword of sorrow pierced during the Passion of your Divine Son and whose soul was filled with unending joy at his glorious Resurrection, intercede for me who invoke you and supplicate your help. (*state your special intentions here*).

V. Pray for us, O most sorrowful Virgin.

R. That we may be made worthy of the promises of Christ.

Let us pray. O Most Loving Lord Jesus, I thank you with humble and loving affection for all the blessings that I have received in abundance from you. The memory of your blessings is stored in me, and especially memorable to me are that you have entrusted me to the care and solicitude of your Blessed Mother and that you have redeemed me from the kingdom of darkness and transferred me to your Kingdom, which is a Kingdom of light, life, and love and of justice, peace, and joy in the Holy Spirit. I also thank you that you have called me to follow you, that you have drawn me closer to you, that you have dissembled and excused my sins and faults, and that you have added thereto many favors to me. O Lord Jesus, I thank you for all the blessings which you have wrought for me and for the whole human race. Amen.

Day 5:   The Prophesy of Simeon

1. The Prophetic Statement of Simeon

Simeon the Prophet received in his arms the Infant Jesus from the arms of Mary. Raising up his eyes and the Infant Jesus to heaven, he offered

God the Son to the God the Father, pronouncing at the same time these words which are recorded in the Gospel of Luke: At last, All-Powerful Master, you may now let your servant go in peace, according to your word; for my eyes have seen your salvation which you have prepared in the sight of all the peoples: a light to reveal you to the nations and the glory of your people Israel. (Lk. 2:29-32).

The Holy Spirit had revealed to Simeon that he would not die until after he had seen the promised Messiah. Thus, Simeon, having seen the Christ, thanked God for fulfilling the promise that God made to him. Simeon then asked that his immortal soul could now be released from the bondage of his mortal body and be allowed to depart in peace to the Lord. Simeon also thanked the Eternal Father for having sent his only begotten Son into the world so that those who wish may enjoy the divine light and not be deprived of the guidance and salvation of the Lord. For Christ is the light revealed to enlighten everyone about the true God and to bring glory to God.

Simeon congratulated Mary on her dignity as the Mother of God and Joseph on his fortune as the putative father of Jesus and as the guardian and protector of Mother and Child on earth. Simeon then blessed them and said to Mary that the Child is destined for the fall and the rise of many people in Israel, that the Child shall be vehemently contradicted, for many shall rise up in opposition against him, that a sword of sorrow shall pierce the heart of Mary, and that the hideous thoughts of many people shall be revealed. Mary and Joseph pondered on the revelation contained in the words of the holy and aged Simeon. (Lk. 2:33-35).

At the prophecy of the priest Simeon, Mary immediately foresaw in a vision the oppositions and contradictions that the Lord Jesus was to endure and his frightful agony and death on the cross. She immediately felt a mystical sword of sorrow pierce her Immaculate Heart at the frightening vision. At the same time, she also foresaw the establishment of the Church, and the eternal glory that her Son would attain for souls. She gave thanks to God silently in her most pure soul.

Although a sword of sorrow immediately pierced her heart at the prophecy of Simeon and at the vision she had seen, nonetheless, Mary remained calm, serene, and tranquil. The prophecy of Simeon and the vision she saw immediately and indelibly impressed themselves upon her memory.

The holy Joseph also saw a vision in which he foresaw the sufferings and death of Jesus. But Joseph was not to be an eye-witness of them during his mortal life. He died about a year before Jesus began his public ministry.

At that time the prophetess Anna came forward to meet the Holy Family; she acknowledged Jesus to be the Incarnate Word, and she gave many thanks to God. And filled with the Holy

Spirit, she spoke of the mysteries of the Child to many people who were expecting the promised Messiah and the redemption of Israel. (Lk. 2:38).

2. Act of Commemoration of the Seven Sorrows of the Blessed Virgin Mary

1. I grieve for you, O Mary most sorrowful, in the affliction of your tender heart at the prophecy of the holy and aged Simeon. Dear Mother, by your heart so afflicted, obtain for me the virtue of humility and the gift of the holy fear of God.
Say 1 Hail Mary.

2. I grieve for you, O Mary most sorrowful, in the anguish of your most affectionate heart during the flight into Egypt and your sojourn there. Dear Mother, by your heart so troubled, obtain for me the virtue of generosity, especially toward the poor, and the gift of piety.
Say 1 Hail Mary.

3. I grieve for you, O Mary most sorrowful, in those anxieties which tried your troubled heart at the loss of your dear Jesus. Dear Mother, by your heart so full of anguish, obtain for me the virtue of chastity and the gift of knowledge.
Say 1 Hail Mary.

4. I grieve for you, O Mary most sorrowful, in the consternation of your heart at meeting Jesus as

he carried his cross. Dear Mother, by your heart so troubled, obtain for me the virtue of patience and the gift of fortitude.
Say 1 Hail Mary.

5. I grieve for you O Mary, most sorrowful, in the martyrdom which your generous heart endured in standing near Jesus in his agony. Dear Mother, by your afflicted heart, obtain for me the virtue of temperance and the gift of counsel.
Say 1 Hail Mary.

6. I grieve for you, O Mary most sorrowful, in the wounding of your compassionate heart, when the side of Jesus was struck by the lance and his Heart was pierced before his body was removed from the cross. Dear Mother, by your heart thus transfixed, obtain for me the virtue of fraternal charity and the gift of understanding.
Say 1 Hail Mary.

7. I grieve for you, O Mary most sorrowful, for the pangs that wrenched your most loving heart at the burial of Jesus. Dear Mother, by your heart sunk in the bitterness of desolation, obtain for me the virtue of diligence and the gift of wisdom.
Say 1 Hail Mary.

V. Pray for us, O most sorrowful Virgin.
R. That we may be made worthy of the promises of Christ.

Let us pray. Grant, we beseech you, O Lord Jesus Christ, that the most Blessed Virgin Mary, your Mother, whose most holy soul was pierced by a sword of sorrow in the hour of your bitter Passion, may intercede for us before the throne of your mercy, now and at the hour of our death. Through you, Jesus Christ, Savior of the world, who lives and reigns with the Father and the Holy Spirit, one God, for ever and ever. Amen.

Day 6:   The Return of the Holy Family to Galilee

1. The Return to Galilee

While in the temple, Mary thanked the Highest King, our Lord and Creator, for his ineffable condescension in favoring her with the graces that she knew she could never merit on her own. She thanked the Lord for the impetuous flood of blessings she has received from him. She asked what she could offer in return to God for all his goodness to her. She acknowledged that she has received her being, existence, and life from God. She said she was overwhelmed by the incomparable mercies and blessings of the Three Divine Persons in one God to her. What thanks could she render in gratitude for their divine immense bounties toward her? What reverence was worthy of the Divine Majesty? What gift would she offer to the Infinite God, since she is only a creature? She has received her soul, her being, and her faculties from the bounteous hands of God. She in turned offered them all to God for his glory. She also acknowledged her indebtedness to God, not only for having given her all the blessings she has received from him, but also for the love with which he has given them to her. She also thanked God who has preserved her from the contagion of sin and who has chosen her to give human form to his only begotten Son, to bear him in her womb, and to nourish her, though she is only a daughter of Adam and a lowly handmaid of the Lord.

She also acknowledged that her heart faints in gratitude whenever she thinks of the Lord's ineffable condescension toward her. She said she will spend her life in giving affections of love to God, for she has nothing else with which to repay the Lord for all the favors he has bestowed upon her. Her heart also rejoices in that that she possesses in her arm a Gift, his only and most beloved Son, who is worthy of the Father's greatness, and she would offer the Father this Divine Gift, who is one in substance with the Father, equal in glory and majesty, and in attributes and perfections with the Father. She would offer to the Eternal Father and Most High God, the gift of his only begotten Son. The Father, she was sure, would accept the Divine and Eternal Gift. She, having received him as God, offers him to the Father as God and Man. Neither she nor any other creature can ever offer the Eternal Father a greater gift, nor can his Divine Majesty ever demand one more precious. In the name of Jesus and in her own name, she offered and presented Christ the Lord to the Eternal Father. She said she is the Mother of his only begotten Son, she gave him human flesh, and she has made him the Brother of all mortals, and as he wishes to be our Redeemer and Teacher, it behooves her to be our advocate, to assume our cause before God and claim assistance for us. She offered Jesus from the depths of heart to the Father of mercies.

When Mary and Joseph had fulfilled all the prescriptions of the law of the Lord, they returned with the Infant Jesus to Galilee, to their own town of Nazareth. (Lk. 2:39). On the way back home, Mary and Joseph thanked the Most High God numerous times for the gift of the Child Jesus. However, she would sometimes shed tears for the sufferings and the death on the cross she knew awaited Jesus in the future. Back at Nazareth, the Child grew and became strong, filled with wisdom; and the favor of God was upon him. (Lk. 2:39-40).

2. Act of Commemoration of the Heavenly Joys of the Blessed Virgin Mary

1. I rejoice with you, O Blessed Virgin Mary, for the joy of yours when, at the moment of your death, your beloved Son and our Lord Jesus Christ received your soul into his arms and when the

whole company of the heavenly angels and saints rejoiced with you on your procession into heaven.

Say 1 Hail Mary.

2. I rejoice with you, O Blessed Virgin Mary, for the joy of yours when your beloved Son and our Lord Jesus Christ led you into paradise and when the whole company of the heavenly angels and saints rejoiced with you on your entrance into heaven.

Say 1 Hail Mary.

3. I rejoice with you, O Blessed Virgin Mary, for the joy of yours when you were assumed body and soul, by your beloved Son and our Lord Jesus Christ, into heaven and when the whole company of the heavenly angels and saints rejoiced with you on your assumption into heaven.

Say 1 Hail Mary.

4. I rejoice with you, O Blessed Virgin Mary, for the joy of yours when the Three Persons of the Most Holy Trinity crowned you Queen of Heaven and Earth and when the whole company of the heavenly angels and saints rejoiced with you on your coronation in heaven.

Say 1 Hail Mary.

5. I rejoice with you, O Blessed Virgin Mary, for the joy of yours when you were seated at the right hand of your beloved Son and our Lord Jesus

Christ and when the whole company of the heavenly saints and angels rejoiced with you on your exaltation in heaven.

Say 1 Hail Mary.

Let us pray. O Most Loving Jesus Christ, pour into my heart and preserve within me the energy and virtue of your most glowing love; may it permeate every fiber of my being, flow evermore through every faculty of my soul, and incorporate me wholly into you eternally. May we, who have invoked the intercession of your most Blessed Mother, be saved from the travails of this life and be granted the rewards of eternal life. To your praise and glory forever and ever. Amen.

Day 7:   Meditations

1. Seek to Preserve Inner Peace

1. The doctrine contained in the presentation of the Lord in the temple is that we should accept from the Lord blessings and adversities, and the sweet and the bitter with equanimity. God spoke to Blessed Virgin Mary, the Mother of his only-Begotten Son, through the prophet Simeon that blessings and joys as well as sufferings and sorrows awaited her. She accepted in good faith both the blessings and the sorrows that accrued to her as the Mother of the Redeemer. There would be a swerving from the path of eternal life if we do not

follow Christ and embrace the cross. Jesus said that if we would be his disciple, we must deny ourselves, take up our cross, and follow him. (Mt. 16:24).

2. How intolerable is the heart toward all that is contrary to its desires! How sentimental is the exclamation and praise that: "The Lord is good all the time; all the time the Lord is good!" However, when the Lord gives us a taste of his cup of suffering, by which the sincerity of our love and praise of God is tried and tested, we ask him: why me, Lord? Seek to preserve interior peace. If transitory labors and pains are accepted with serenity of heart, they bless the soul and the soul receives consolation and blessings from God.

3. If people disappoint you, or if temptation and trouble assail you, be not disturbed or disheartened; ask God for help and apply the graces given you by him to the situation. Confide in the protection of the Most High and press onward trusting in Jesus and Mary. Whenever tribulation comes to you, fervently exclaim: The Lord is my light and my help; whom shall I fear? The Lord is the stronghold of my life; before whom shall I shrink? When evil-doers draw near to devour my flesh, it is they, my enemies and foes, who stumble and fall. Jesus Christ is a Father, a Brother, and a Friend to me. I have the Blessed Virgin Mary as my Mother and my Queen. They will assist me and take care of me in my affliction. Amen.

2. Act of Praise of the Blessed Virgin Mary

O Blessed Virgin Mary, Immaculate Conception, beautiful and full of grace, I join with the angels and the saints in rendering thanks and gratitude to God for all the graces, favors, and privileges that he has bestowed upon you. Your name is powerful and magnificent. Those who invoke you with devout affection receive most abundant graces. Those who honor and pronounce your name with reverence are consoled and vivified. Those who call upon your name with faith find the remedy for their evils, the treasures for their enrichment, and the light which guide them to heaven. Your most holy name is terrible to the powers of darkness. It has crushed the head of the serpent, and won glorious victories over the princes and powers of darkness.

I acknowledge, honor, and venerate you as the Mother of the Incarnate Word and as the Queen of Heaven and Earth. I venerate your most holy name. I acknowledge, honor, and venerate you for all your sorrows and sufferings you endured in union with your Son and our Lord Jesus Christ. I give thanks to the Most Blessed Trinity for all the special graces, gifts, and privileges granted to you. O precious and priceless Pearl of Heaven, conceived without sin, bestow upon me the fragrance of sanctity! O sublime Mother of mothers, who excels in dignity and grandeur, fill me with your benediction and holy love! O Blessed joy of the angels and the just! Grant me, by your special prerogatives and privileges and by your sweet and holy name, more abundant merits and graces.

O Blessed Virgin Mary, Mother of God and my Mother, by the merits of the precious Blood of Jesus and by the merits of your sufferings, obtain for me the forgiveness of my sins, the remission of the punishments and pains due to my sins, the perfect amendment of my life, and the admission of my soul one day to the eternal glory of heaven. Amen.

V. O Mary, conceived without sin.

R. Pray for us who have recourse to you.

Let us pray. O Lord and God, who seeks in me only what is pure, holy, and perfect, may the Most Blessed Trinity be praised and magnified for the gracious blessings granted to the Blessed Virgin Mary. Through Christ our Lord. Amen.

WEEK 2: THE SECOND SORROW OF THE BLESSED VIRGIN MARY - THE FLIGHT TO EGYPT

When the Magi had departed, an angel of the Lord appeared to Joseph in a dream and said, "Rise, take the child and his mother, and flee to Egypt, and remain there until I tell you. Behold, Herod is about to search for the child to destroy him." Joseph rose, took the child and his mother by night and went to Egypt, and remained there until the death of Herod. (Mt. 2:13-15a).

Day 8:   The Arrival of the Magi in Judah

1.   The Visit of the Magi

"When Jesus was born in Bethlehem of Judea, in the days of King Herod, behold, Magi from the east arrived in Jerusalem, saying, "Where is the newborn king of the Jews? We saw his star at its rising and have come to do him homage." (Mt. 2:1-2). Their inquiry came to the ears of King Herod who, at that time, reigned in Judea and lived in Jerusalem. When King Herod heard that the Messiah King had been born, he was greatly troubled, and all Jerusalem with him. Assembling all the chief priests and the scribes of the people, he inquired of them where the Messiah was to be born. They said to him: In Bethlehem of Judea, for thus it has been written through the prophet: And you,

Bethlehem, land of Judah, are by no means least among the rulers of Judah; since from you shall come a ruler, who is to shepherd my people Israel. (Mt. 2:3-6). The wicked King Herod became panic-stricken at the thought that a legitimate Claimant to the throne should have been born and that the Heir-Apparent to the throne was outside of the lineage of Herod. He felt much disturbed, troubled, and outraged by this report.

Having ascertained from the chiefs priests and scribes that the Christ was to be born in Bethlehem, King Herod then called the Magi secretly and ascertained from them the time they saw the star. He then sent them to Bethlehem and, with covert malice, said to them: Go and search diligently for the Child. When you have found him, bring me word, that I too may go and do him homage. After their audience with King Herod they set out. (Mt. 2:7-9). Herod immediately began to plot from that very moment to destroy Jesus.

The Magi then departed, leaving the hypocritical king ill at ease and in great disturbance of mind at such indisputable signs of the coming of the legitimate King of Israel into the world. Although he could have eased his mind in regard to his sovereignty by the thought that a recently born infant could not be enthroned so very soon, yet human nature is so fragile and insecure that it can be overthrown even by an infant or by the mere threat or thought of far-off danger.

When they left the palace of King Herod, the star that the Magi had seen at its rising appeared before them again and preceded them. The Magi were overjoyed at seeing the star. (Mt. 2:10-11). The star led them until it stopped over the Cave of the Nativity wherein the Infant Jesus was with Mary, his Mother, and with Joseph.

When the three kings of the East first entered the Cave of the Nativity, they were for a considerable length of time overwhelmed with awe and wonder at their first sight of Mother and Child and at the heavenly light that glowed around the Holy Family. They prostrated themselves upon the earth, and worshiped the Infant King, acknowledging him as true God and true Man, and as the Savior of the human race. Mary and Joseph glorified the Lord with new songs of praise because his name was beginning to be known and adored among the Gentiles. (Ps. 86:9).

The three kings opened their treasures and offered him gifts of gold, frankincense, and myrrh. (Mt. 2:11). Mary received the gifts from them on behalf of the Holy Family, and thanked them for the gifts. And having been warned in a dream to not return to Herod, the three kings from the East departed for their respective countries by another route. (Mt. 2:12). On their departure from Bethlehem the star which had guided them to the place of the Nativity of Jesus re-appeared in order to guide them back to their different countries. It guided them by a different route to the place where they had first gathered to commence their journey to Palestine. From their mustering point, each of the three kings then separated and went to their respective countries with gratitude to God for their safe journey to and from Palestine and for mission accomplished. The star of Christ that had guided them then disappeared from human sight forever so that people would not begin to worship the star itself rather than the Christ himself. In addition, it had accomplished its purpose, namely to guide the Magi to the Christ of God from and back to their respective countries.

2. Act of Reparation to the Sorrowful and Immaculate Heart of Mary

O most glorious Virgin Mary, Mother of God and our Mother, look with pity upon us poor sinners, who, afflicted with so many miseries surrounding us in this life, feel ourselves cut to the heart by the many horrible insults and blasphemies which we are often constrained to hear uttered against you, O Immaculate Virgin. Oh, how these impious sayings offend the infinite Majesty of God the Father, the divinity and humanity of Jesus Christ his only begotten Son, and the goodness and charity of God the Holy Spirit! How they provoke his anger, and give us cause to fear the terrible effects of his vengeance! If the sacrifice of our lives could avail against such outrages and blasphemies, very willingly would we make it, for we desire, most holy Mother, to love and honor you with all our hearts, such being the will of God. And because we love you, we will do whatever is within our power to make you loved and honored by all. O Mother of pity, consoler of the afflicted, accept this act of reparation which we offer to you, in the name of Jesus, and on behalf of those who, not knowing what they say, impiously blaspheme you. Obtain for them from God their conversion. And by your glorious compassion, power, and mercy, may they one day join with us in proclaiming you, O Immaculate Virgin, O most compassionate Mother of God, most blessed among women. Amen.

V. Pray for us, O most sorrowful Virgin.

R. That we may be made worthy of the promises of Christ.

Let us pray. Let intercession be made for us, we beseech you, O Lord Jesus Christ, now and at the hour of our death, before the throne of your mercy, by the Blessed Virgin Mary, your Mother, whose most holy soul was pierced by a sword of sorrow in the hour of your bitter Passion. We ask this through you, Jesus Christ, Savior of the world, who lives and reigns with the Father and the Holy Spirit, one God, forever and ever. Amen.

Day 9:   The Escape of the Holy Family from Herod

1. The Journey of the Holy Family to Egypt

After the Magi had departed from Bethlehem to their respective countries, an angel of the Lord appeared to Joseph in a dream and said to him: "Rise, take the child and his mother, and flee to Egypt, and remain there until I tell you. Behold, Herod is about to search for the child to destroy him." Joseph rose, took the child and his mother by night and went to Egypt, and remained there until the death of Herod. (Mt. 2:13-15a). God allowed the Holy Family to flee to Egypt because the time for the manifestation of Christ as the Son of God and of the power of God had not yet come. God also allowed the Holy Family to flee to Egypt in order to fulfill the prophecies of Prophet Isaiah that the Lord shall visit Egypt and the idols of Egypt shall tremble at his presence and that the heart of the Egyptians shall melt (Is. 19:1). This ancient prophecy was thus fulfilled when the Holy Family entered Egypt.

The journey from Nazareth to Egypt was long and difficult. It was winter-time, and they had little protection from the cold; but they suffered it all for the sake of God. The road from Palestine to Egypt was a desert, and they had no night-shelter since the desert was all open air. Joseph walked on foot, while Mary with the Infant Jesus in her arms

31

rode on a donkey; sometimes, however, she would, with the Infant Jesus on her shoulders, walk on foot. The Holy Family suffered much on the journey on account of the distance, the winter cold, the heat of the sun, the lack of shelter, hunger, and thirst. Mary felt very deeply for the sufferings of her Infant Son, Jesus, and for that of her holy spouse, Joseph. On his part, Joseph was deeply saddened because he was unable to ease the hardships of his legal Son, Jesus, and of his holy spouse, Mary.

The desert road was also dangerous because of robbers and other hoodlums. But God protected the Holy Family from all the dangers of the desert.

Mary, with the Infant Jesus in her arms, would sometimes seat herself on the earth and, with her husband, eat of the food they brought with them. She also nursed the Infant Jesus. In order to provide them with some shelter from the hot, desert sun and the freezing, winter cold, Joseph, however little and humble it might be, formed a sort of tent for the Infant Jesus and Mary with his cloak and some sticks. She offered up her hardships, those of Jesus, and those of Joseph to the Eternal Father for the salvation of souls.

In addition to the sufferings caused by their fatigue, hunger, and thirst, they also experienced storms of cold wind, which blew against them with fury accompanied with rain storms and which soaked them; and they were unable to dry themselves. Although she tried to protect the Infant in her arms as much as she could, nonetheless, she could not prevent him from the inclemency of the weather. To shield the Holy Family against the inclemency of the weather, God the Father would send his angels to surround the Holy Family in the form of a resplendent and beautiful globe round about and over the Incarnate God, his Mother, and Joseph, her most holy spouse. The angels did this several times during the journey of the Holy Family through the desert.

Soon the Holy Family ran out of food. They began to suffer great hunger. And there was no natural means of renewing their supply of food and water. Mary, therefore, prayed to the Eternal Father to look upon his only begotten Son and send them food and water so that their natural life would be sustained and so that they would serve his Majesty for the salvation of the human race. The Lord God then commanded his angels and they brought to the Holy Family loaves of the most delicious bread, well-seasoned fruits, and a large container of the most delicious drink. Then all of them together sang hymns of praise and thanksgiving to the Lord, who gives food to all creatures at opportune times, in order that the poor may eat and be filled – the poor whose eyes and hopes are fixed upon his kingly providence and bounty. (Ps. 136:25). God permitted the necessity of food and drink to afflict the Holy Family so as to let people know that he will assist all who call upon him in their times of need and they will find his heavenly assistance readily available.

Finally, the Holy Family reached Egypt. The angels did not conduct the Holy Family through a direct route to Heliopolis, the then capital of Egypt. They were conducted by the angels, according to the command of the Most High, in a roundabout way, so that they might pass through as many towns and cities as possible in Egypt, where God wished his miracles and blessings to be wrought for the good of the Egyptians. In total, the journey from Palestine to Heliopolis, the present day Cairo, took the Holy Family sixty days to complete, and the distance was about two hundred and sixty miles or four hundred and eighteen kilometers.

2. Act of Consolation and Compassion to the Mother of Sorrows

O Most Holy Virgin, Immaculate Mother of God, you endured the long, tedious, and difficult journey with the Infant Jesus and your most holy Spouse, St. Joseph, to Egypt. You suffered, with an overwhelming grief, the Passion, Crucifixion, and Death of your divine Son. You co-operated in the benefit of my redemption by your innumerable afflictions and by offering to the Eternal Father his only-begotten Son as a sacrifice and victim of propitiation for my sins. I thank you for the unconditional love which led you to deprive yourself of the Fruit of your womb, Jesus, true God and true Man, to save me, a sinner. O make use of the unfailing intercession of your sorrows with the Father and the Son and the Holy Spirit so that I may amend my life and never again crucify my loving Redeemer and so that, persevering till death in his grace, I may obtain eternal life. Amen.

V. Honor, glory, and love to our Divine Lord Jesus.

R. And to the Holy and Immaculate Mother of God.

Let us pray. O Lord Jesus Christ, by the overwhelming grief the Blessed Virgin Mary experienced when she witnessed your crucifixion and death, look upon me with eyes of compassion and awaken in my heart a tender commiseration for those sufferings, as well as a sincere detestation of my sins, in order that, being disengaged from all undue affections for the passing joys of this earth, I may long for the eternal Jerusalem, and that henceforth all my thoughts and all my actions may be directed toward this one intention. Honor, glory, and love to you, our divine Lord Jesus, forever and ever. Amen.

Day 10:   The Massacre of the Holy Innocents

1. The Massacre of the Holy Innocents

Unbeknownst to the wicked King Herod, the Magi had departed by a different route to their respective home countries and the Infant Jesus, Mary, and Joseph had escaped from Palestine to Egypt. Meanwhile, Herod was still awaiting the return of the Magi to give him a report about the location of the Infant King so that he would immediately send soldiers to take the life of the Infant, Jesus. Although he trusted in his own cunning, nonetheless, he forgot that God sees all things and knows the secrets of the heart. (Ps. 44:22). After he had waited for several days, Herod became increasingly anxious and angst that the Magi were not returning to bring him news about the Infant King. He then sent emissaries to Bethlehem because that was where the scriptures said the Redeemer would be born and because he, too, had sent the Magi to Bethlehem.

The emissaries of Herod then went to Bethlehem, reconnoitered the town, and reported back to King Herod. They informed him that the Magi had indeed reached and lodged in Bethlehem; however, the Eastern Kings had since returned to their respective countries by a different route. When Herod realized that he had been outsmarted by the Magi, he was livid with anger. (Mt. 2:16). The Bible says that with the sincere the Lord shows himself sincere, but to the cunning, he outsmarts them in their cunning (Ps. 18:27).

He then ordered his spies to go and thoroughly search for Mary, the Infant Jesus, and Joseph. However, the Lord, who knew of the wicked plan of King Herod, had since commanded the Holy Family to flee from Palestine to Egypt. Moreover, the Lord had so concealed their escape to Egypt and their whereabouts from everyone such that not a single soul on the face of the earth knew of the whereabouts of the Holy Family.

Unable to find the Holy Family, the henchmen of Herod reported back that they could not find Mary, the Infant King, and Joseph. In addition, they also told Herod that there was not any man, woman, or child under the face of the earth who knew of the whereabouts of Mary, the Infant King, and Joseph. This double negative news to Herod was like adding gasoline to an already raging fire.

Herod considered the Infant King, Christ the Lord, as a threat to his own dynasty of Herod. Having realized that he was no match to the sagacity of the Wise Men and having failed to locate the whereabouts of the Holy Family, Herod concocted a plan to use his royal power to murder all the children under two years of age in Bethlehem and its environ. For in that way he thought that the King of the Jews, the Heir-Apparent to his throne who was recently born there, would inevitably be murdered among them. He then ordered some troops to go and kill all the children less than two years old in Bethlehem and its environs. The command of Herod was then executed and the whole country was thrown into mourning, especially the wailing and tears of the parents and relatives of the innocent children who had been murdered by him. Thus, a voice was heard in Ramah: wailing and great mourning. Rachel was crying for her children. She refused to be consoled, because they were no more. (Mt. 2:18). A great number of children were murdered by Herod. These Holy Innocents were the first to shed their blood for Christ. Mary prayed for the repose of their soul and for the consolation of their parents.

2. Intercessory Prayer to the Sorrowful Mother for Those in Danger of Death

O Blessed Virgin Mary, chosen from among all creatures according to the good pleasure of the Most Blessed Trinity to be the Mother of the Incarnate Word. O Queen of angels and mortals, you are ever-ready to guide and assist souls to eternal life. You have at your disposal so many privileges and so many graces of help solely for the benefit of mortals. O Mother of sorrows, so great a grief is caused you by people who fail to call upon you and who refuse you the glory of saving their souls. You are most punctual and liberal in coming to the aid of souls. We beseech you, on behalf of souls who are in danger of death and who shall die today, especially those who are devoted to you, to come to their assistance, to protect them from their last temptations, and to save them from eternal damnation. And by your special powers and privileges before the Throne of Most Blessed Trinity and by the merits of the precious Blood of Jesus Christ, may the Merciful and Compassionate Father, who is worthy of all reverence and praise, bend his clemency toward them, forgive them their sins, and grant them eternal life. Amen.

Say 3 Hail Marys.

Let us pray. O Jesus, remember all the dread and sorrow you endured when Pilate pronounced on you a sentence of death; when the godless soldiers laid the heavy cross on your shoulders, and fastened you thereon with rude and blunted nails, cruelly stretching your sacred Limbs so that all your sacred Bones could be numbered. I beseech you, vouchsafe to pronounce a merciful sentence on me in the day of judgment, and deliver souls who shall spend their last day on earth today from eternal damnation and bring them to the joys of your eternal kingdom. Amen.

Day 11: The Arrival of the Holy Family in Egypt

1. The Holy Family Arrives in Egypt

Egypt was much given to idolatry and superstitions. Every city, town, and countryside was full of idols and steeped in demonic worship. In order to deliver and enlighten these Egyptians who were living in the shadow of death (Lk. 1:79) and in order that they might see the light of God (Is. 9:2), the Most High ordained that Jesus Christ, the Sun of Justice, (Mal. 4:2), should, shortly after his birth, appear in Egypt in the arms of his most blessed Mother and that he should journey and pass through Egypt, illumining everywhere in it by the power of his divine light.

Thus, whenever the Infant Jesus, with his Mother and Joseph, entered any city, town, or countryside in Egypt, the demons would flee to the abyss of hell, the idols would crash to the ground, and the altars erected in honor of the demons would fall to the ground in pieces. The Egyptian people were astounded at these inexplicable happenings. However, among the more learned of them, ever since the sojourn of Jeremiah in Egypt, an ancient tradition was current that a King of the Jews would come and that the temples of the idols would be destroyed. Yet of this prophecy the common people had no knowledge, nor did the learned know how and when it was to be fulfilled. According to Isaiah: The people who walked in darkness have seen a great light; those who lived in a land of deep darkness on them a great light has shone. (Isa, 9:2). Egypt and the rest of North Africa have produced many saints, including St. Anthony of Egypt, St. Augustine of

Hippo (present day Algiers, Algeria), and other hermits and saints since the sojourn of the Holy Family to Egypt. There is to this day a fountain near Cairo from which Mary drew water for herself and the Infant Jesus, and for the washing of his clothes.

2. Special Intention Prayer to the Mother of Sorrows

O Blessed Virgin Mary, the chosen one of the Most Blessed Trinity and whose name was chosen by the Eternal Father himself! Your name is powerful and magnificent. I invoke you with devout affection and humbly beseech you to grant me abundant graces of mind, soul, and body. I honor your most sweet name and pronounce it with reverence. Grant me consolation and strength, remedy for all my spiritual and corporal ills, your treasures for my enrichment, and the virtues and devotions which shall guide me to heaven. Your name is terrible against the power of hell; crush the head of the serpent for me and win glorious victories for me over the princes of hell. By your love for the Most High console, alleviate, and enliven me, and by your natural compassion, procure for me all corporeal and spiritual blessings, especially the following special intentions of mine. (*state your intentions here*).

I praise and bless eternally our Lord, who in his infinite mercy chose you as his Mother, and as

41

the treasurer of all his great blessings and sacraments. Be mindful of me, your child, before our Lord and God, that he may lead me in peace through this exile to the security of the eternal peace which we hope for, and that through you I may merit the vision of his Divinity, which is the glory of the saints. Remember also, O Mother of God and Queen of all creation, all the members of my family; pray to the Most High for us so that we may serve the God and Father of our Lord Jesus Christ in holiness and faithfulness all the days of our life. All generations call you blessed, and all the nations recognize and praise your grace and beauty! The earth is made illustrious by your birth. Graciously condescend toward me and bless me. I bless and magnify the Most High God for his blessings and benefits to you. Amen.

V. Pray for us, O most sorrowful Virgin.

R. That we may be made worthy of the promises of Christ.

Let us pray. O Most Loving Lord Jesus, I thank you with humble and loving affection for all the blessings that I have received in abundance from you. The memory of your blessings is stored in me, and especially memorable to me are that you have entrusted me to the care and solicitude of your Blessed Mother, that you have redeemed me from the kingdom of darkness and transferred me to your Kingdom, which is a Kingdom of light, life, and love and of justice, peace, and joy in the

Holy Spirit. I also thank you that you have called me to follow you, that you have drawn me closer to you, that you have dissembled and excused my sins and faults, and that you have added thereto many favors to me. O Lord Jesus, I thank you for all the blessings which you have wrought for me and for the whole human race. Amen.

Day 12:   The Life and Miracles of the Holy Family in Egypt

1. The Holy Family in Egypt

When they arrived in Heliopolis, present day Cairo, Joseph purchased a three bedroom house, and they lived there. Upon entering the house, Mary with her divine Son and Joseph, prostrated themselves on the ground in profound humility and lovingly thanked the Most High for having brought them safely to Egypt and for having secured the house for them after their prolonged and laborious journey to Egypt. Having performed these acts of devotion, Mary then proceeded to clean, arrange, and put the house in order. She asked her new neighbors for help with their instruments, household utensils, and utilities for this purpose. Mary could have commanded her guardian angels to arrange and put the house in order for her; however, she chose to do it herself so that she could earn more merits in heaven. And she asked her new neighbors to assist her with their utensils and utilities so that God would use the assistance provided to her by these neighbors as a means to bless the neighbors a hundredfold, which the Lord did.

For the first three days of their sojourn in Heliopolis, the Holy Family relied on the generosity of their neighbors for food, cooking utensils, and other basic necessities of life. Then, soon enough, Joseph set up a carpentry shop in the city and he began to earn some wages by his work. Then he made a humble couch for Mary and a cradle for the Infant Jesus; while he himself had as a resting place only the bare ground; for the house was as yet without any furniture until by his own labor he succeeded in making some household furniture for the convenience of all three of them. Each of the furniture made by Joseph was so unique and perfect that his reputation as one of the best carpenters in town soon spread around and about that there was no shortage of demands for his products.

On her part, Mary assisted Joseph in providing food on the table and in paying the house bills. She was taught needlework and crocheting by one of the women who was a neighbor to her. In no time, she became so perfect that the reputation of her par excellence skills soon spread around and about that there was no shortage of demand for her work such as clothing, embroidery, quilting, etc. She also busied herself with her household chores such as cleaning the house, cooking meals for Joseph, and washing and taking care of herself and her Infant Son, Jesus. Joseph, in addition to his work at the shop, also helped Mary in looking after Baby Jesus. Whenever he carried Jesus in his arms, Joseph would not only give thanks to God but he would also forget all the hardships of his work and find his work easier and more fulfilling.

Mary adored the Infant Jesus as God and, at the same time, caressed him with tenderness as a Mother would do to her child. It is impossible to conceive how she balanced perfectly her obligations to the Infant God as from a creature to her Creator, looking upon him as the Son of the Eternal Father, King of kings, and Lord of lords, the Maker and Preserver of all the universe; and, at the same time, her obligations as Mother to her Infant Child, serving him and nursing him. In performing these two grave duties she was entirely inflamed with love, and her whole being was filled with heroic acts of admiration, praise, and affection for her Divine Son.

She also did not miss her spiritual exercises such as her prayers and contemplations. She did not expect God to perform miracles for her for those things which she could obtain by her natural faculties, by natural means, by diligence, and by the labor of her hand. In this, she wishes to leave a moral lesson for people so that we may not God for miracles for those things that we can accomplish by ourselves or ask God for miracles for our convenience and comfort rather than out of true necessity. Thus, she asked the Eternal Father not for miracles but for the Eternal Father to provide, by natural means and sometimes by divine intervention, sustenance and the necessities of life for her divine Son, for her holy spouse, Joseph, and for herself.

Mary and Joseph also spoke to the people about the true and living God, the spiritual paths to eternal life, and the Incarnate Word. Mary impressed upon their minds the 10 Commandments of God, showed them the manner of adoring and worshipping God, and how they were to expect the redemption of the human race. Mary and Joseph also cured some of their sick. The reports of the mysterious healing of the sick at the hands of Mary so rapidly spread that within a short space of time an immense number of people were coming to see Jesus, Mary, and Joseph. God also granted healing powers to Joseph; however, Mary did most of the preaching, exhortations, and healings. A great number of people were converted. Whenever Mary listened to and healed those who came to her, she held in her arms the Infant Jesus. She spoke to each one of them in the manner suitable to the person's capacity for understanding the doctrine of eternal life. She enlightened them concerning God and made them understand that there is only one God. She explained to them the several articles of truth pertaining to the Creation and Redemption of the world.

Their life in Egypt, however, was not without persecutions. For example, some blamed for the fall and destruction of the idols in the city. There was also once when a group of scoundrels in the city, at the instigation of the fallen angels, decided to kill the Holy Family. Some elders in the city, however, counseled against taking the life of Jesus, Mary, and Joseph. These elders counseled that the ancestors of these Strangers in their midst once sojourned in Egypt many centuries ago. When Pharaoh wanted to harm the ancestors of this Family, all the firstborns of the Egyptians, both of people and of animals, died mysteriously. If the people of the city did not want their own firstborns to die mysteriously as well, they should leave these Strangers from Israel alone. The Holy Family bore the persecutions they faced with patience, humility, and faith in God.

2. Act of Commemoration of the Seven Sorrows of the Blessed Virgin Mary

1. O Most Blessed Virgin Mary, I beseech you, by the merits of the sorrows that pierced your Sorrowful and Immaculate Heart at the prophecy of Simeon and by your most spotless purity, to convert sinners and bring more souls to Christ. Amen.
Say 1 Hail Mary.

2. O Most Sacred Virgin Mary, I beseech you, by the merits of the sorrows that pierced your Sorrowful and Immaculate Heart when you were informed that Herod was seeking the life of your dear Child and you had to flee with the Infant King and with St. Joseph to Egypt and by your most perfect motherly love, to save the dying and bring them to the rewards of eternal joy. Amen.
Say 1 Hail Mary.

3. O Most Loving Virgin Mary, I beseech you, by the merits of the sorrows that pierced your Sorrowful and Immaculate Heart at the loss of the Child Jesus for three days until at last he was found in the temple and by your most gentle and profound humility, to free the souls in purgatory, especially those who are most in need of your mercy. Amen.
Say 1 Hail Mary.

4. O Most Holy Virgin Mary, I beseech you, by the virtues of the sorrows that pierced your Sorrowful and Immaculate Heart at the pitiful sight of your most holy and innocent Child Jesus and our Lord and by your most holy and blessed life, to assist priests so that they may celebrate the Sacrifice of the Holy Mass with reverence and devotion and to assist all married couples and single people to live out faithfully the vocation to which God has called them to follow him. Amen.
Say 1 Hail Mary.

5. O Most Kind Virgin Mary, I beseech you, by the virtues of the sorrows that pierced your Sorrowful and Immaculate Heart at the crucifixion and death of Jesus and by your sorrows and sufferings, to assist communicants to receive Holy Communion worthily and with reverence. Amen.
Say 1 Hail Mary.

6. O Most Compassionate Virgin Mary, I beseech you, by the virtues of the sorrows that pierced your Sorrowful and Immaculate Heart at the thrust of the lance into the sacred Side of Jesus and the taking down of his sacred Body from the cross into your virginal arms and by the merits of your dignity as the Mother of God, to cleanse me from every stain of sin and obtain for me the perfect amendment of my life. Amen.
Say 1 Hail Mary.

7. O Most Faithful Virgin Mary, I beseech you, by the virtues of the sorrows that pierced your Sorrowful and Immaculate Heart at the burial of Jesus and by your most holy and heavenly love of God, to obtain for me an abundant increase of all merits, the forgiveness of my sins, and the salvation of my soul. Amen.
Say 1 Hail Mary.

V. O Sorrowful and Immaculate Heart of Mary.
R. Pray for us who have recourse to you.

Let us pray. I praise you, O Good Jesus, through your sweetest Heart, for the holy and blessed life of your Blessed Mother. I humbly beseech you, by the merits of your precious Blood and by the merits of her sorrows, to save souls and bring them to the joys of paradise. Amen.

Day 13: The Return of the Holy Family from Egypt to Nazareth

1. The Return of the Holy Family to Nazareth

The Holy Family stayed in Egypt for seven years. Thus, when the Child Jesus completed his seventh year, the angel of the Lord appeared to Joseph in a dream and told him to take the Child and his Mother and return to the land of Israel, for Herod and those who sought the life of the Child were dead. (Mt. 2:19). It was necessary for them to return to Israel in order to fulfill what had been spoken by the Lord through the prophet, "Out of Egypt I have called my son."[2]

Joseph immediately awoke and notified Mary of the will of the heavenly Father. Thereupon, they began to prepare for their journey back to Israel without delay. They distributed their furniture to the poor. They gave their holy and consecrated house to a devout and pious neighbor. All their

---

[2] Hos. 11:1; Mt. 2:15.

friends, neighbors, and acquaintances as well as the playmates of Jesus were overwhelmed with sadness at the news of their departure. For in addition to the many healings and conversions to the way of the Lord they had experienced favorably from the Holy Family, the Egyptians also experienced divine peace, prosperity, and protection of God in their midst. Thus, upon the announcement that the God-Man and his earthly family were leaving their midst, the Egyptians immediately began to feel sadness in their hearts. The Sun of Justice, who had arisen in their midst with healing in his hands (Mal. 4:2), who had dispersed their darkness, and who had brightened their life and their land was setting forth for the land of Israel. It was with much difficulty that they allowed the Holy Family to leave. Joseph used all his persuasive powers to convince them that it was time to depart back to their homeland. If the divine power had not intervened, the Egyptians would not have allowed the Holy Family to depart from their midst. The Holy Family departed Egypt in the company of angels. Mary sat on the donkey with Jesus, who was seven years old then, while Joseph walked afoot, closely following Jesus and Mary.

In departing Egypt, the Holy Family once more passed through many Egyptian towns and villages so as to bestow graces and blessings to as many people as they could. As they passed through various towns and villages, the news of their departure spread quickly around and about, and all the sick, the afflicted, and the disconsolate lined up on the streets the Holy Family would pass, and they were all cured. Many demons were cast out from people. All those who came to see the Holy Family off left their presence enlightened with divine truths, filled with divine grace, and wounded with divine love.

The Holy Family entered the desert through the way which they had come seven years earlier. They again suffered difficulties similar to those they suffered on their hastened departure from Palestine; for the Lord permitted them to undergo hardships and difficulties in the journey in order to afford Joseph and Mary occasions to earn merits in heaven and to provide them with relief and assistance. Sometimes, the Child Jesus himself would tell the angels to provide sustenance for the Holy Family. Oftentimes, Joseph, in order that he might become more aware of the divinity of Christ, was permitted to hear Jesus speak to the angels in his heart and to see the angels, who readily obeyed Jesus and procured what was needed for the preservation of the Holy Family. This greatly encouraged and consoled Joseph in his sorrow and anxiety for the King and the Queen of heaven. At other times, the Divine Child would make use of his Omnipotence and create out of a crumb of bread all that was necessary to supply for their wants.

When they arrived at the boundary of Palestine, Joseph was informed that Archelaus had succeeded Herod his father in the government of Judea (Mt. 2:22). Concerned that Archelaus had not only inherited the throne of his father, but also the cruelty of his father, Joseph passed through another route, without going through Jerusalem, to get to Nazareth, their home, for Jesus was to be called a Nazarene. They found their humble house all in good condition. Upon entering their abode, Jesus, Mary, and Joseph immediately prostrated themselves on the ground to God the Eternal Father in adoration thanking him for having saved them from the cruelty of Herod, for having protected them from dangers during their long and arduous journeys to and fro the land of Egypt, for having preserved and protected them in their sojourn in Egypt, and for having brought them back safely to their home country and to their humble home.

2. Act of Commemoration of the Joys of the Blessed Virgin Mary

1. I rejoice with you, O most resplendent Virgin Mary, for the stream of graces which flows forth to you from the Heart of the Most Holy Trinity by reason of your most blessed predestination as the chosen Mother of God.

2. I rejoice with you, O most amiable Virgin Mary, for the stream of graces which flows forth to

you from the Heart of the Most Holy Trinity by reason of your Immaculate Conception.

3. I rejoice with you, O most radiant Virgin Mary, for the stream of graces which flows forth to you from the Heart of the Most Holy Trinity by reason of your most blessed life.

4. I rejoice with you, O most holy Virgin Mary, for the stream of graces which flows forth to you from the Heart of the Most Holy Trinity by reason of your glorious and virginal Motherhood.

5. I rejoice with you, O most chaste Virgin Mary, for the stream of graces which flows forth to you from the Heart of the Most Holy Trinity by reason of your holy betrothal.

6. I rejoice with you, O most noble Virgin Mary, for the stream of graces which flows forth to you from the Heart of the Most Holy Trinity by reason of the life and ministry of Jesus.

7. I rejoice with you, O most loving Virgin Mary, for the stream of graces which flows forth to you from the Heart of the Most Holy Trinity by reason of the bitter Passion and Death of Jesus.

8. I rejoice with you, O most compassionate Virgin Mary, for the stream of graces which flows forth to you from the Heart of the Most Holy Trinity by reason of the Resurrection of Jesus.

9. I rejoice with you, O most admirable Virgin Mary, for the stream of graces which flows forth to you from the Heart of the Most Holy Trinity by

reason of the Descent of the Holy Spirit on you and on the Apostles on Pentecost Day.

10. I rejoice with you, O most kind Virgin Mary, for the stream of graces which flows forth to you from the Heart of the Most Holy Trinity by reason of your Assumption body and soul in Heaven.

11. I rejoice with you, O most merciful Virgin Mary, for the stream of graces which flows forth to you from the Heart of the Most Holy Trinity by reason of your Coronation as Queen of Heaven and Earth.

12. I rejoice with you, O most sacred Virgin Mary, for the stream of graces which flows forth to you from the Heart of the Most Holy Trinity by reason of your exaltation above the choirs of angels and the saints.

V. O Mary, conceived without sin.

R. Pray for us who have recourse to you.

Let us pray. O Most Holy Trinity, have mercy on me and deign to pardon all my sins. I beseech you by all the love of the Sacred Heart of Jesus and the Immaculate Heart of Mary that you would vouchsafe to grant me that perfection with which God the Son stood arrayed in the presence of God the Father when he ascended on high to enter into his glory. Through his sinless and spotless humanity render my soul pure and free from every sin; through his most glorious Divinity endow and adorn it with every virtue; and through the virtue of that love, which has forever united his supreme Divinity to his immaculate Humanity, furnish it befittingly with your best gifts. Amen.

Day 14:   Meditations

1.   Trust in Divine Providence

1.   Miracles do happen. However, we should not expect God to perform a divine miracle for us when we can procure through the work of our hands and through natural means the provisions for the preservation and sustenance of our life. Our domestic work and our legitimate means of livelihood profit not only our body but also our soul; for by performing our work and fulfilling our obligations, we increase our merits in heaven. Do your work, and the Lord will supply for the needs that your income cannot adequately meet. When has the Lord ever failed those who hoped in his assistance? (Ps. 18:31). When has he ever turned away his countenance from his afflicted and helpless children? We are all brothers and sisters of God's only begotten Son, Jesus Christ. We are also all God's children, co-heirs with Jesus Christ, his Son, and children of the Blessed Mother, Mary ever-Virgin. The arms of the Lord are ever opened toward us so that we may always receive blessings and assistance from him.

2.   Trust in God and acknowledge him as our heavenly Father who is willing to provide for his

children, and who will nourish and sustain us in all our necessities without fail. Secured in this confidence, Mary was not alarmed in her prolonged journey to and exile in Egypt. Since she trusted in the Lord, he provided for her and her family in the time of her need. The Lord is an ever-present help in time of need. (Ps. 46:1). Oh you who trust in Divine Providence, neither afflict yourself in the time of need nor neglect the worship of God in order to make provision for material needs. When you have played your part, confide in the Lord; hope patiently, even when help seems delayed. It will always be at hand at a time when it will do you the most good and when the paternal love of God can manifest itself most openly to you and others.

3. Trust in Divine Providence. Let the will of the Lord be your only delight and joy. Let not your exterior occupations or your internal dispositions impede or divert you from your religious devotions and exercises. Human life is interwoven with prosperity and adversity. Those who know the Lord trust in him, and those who trust in him have knowledge of the goodness of God. In addition, the arms of Our Blessed Mother, Mary, are ever stretched out toward us and her hands are ever opened so that we can come to her and receive blessings and assistance from her.

4. The Magi offered great gifts to the King of kings, and they did so with great affection. Their gifts were most acceptable to God. There are very

few people in the world today who use well their temporal riches and offer them to their God and Creator with the generosity and love of these holy Kings. The poor of the Lord, so numerous in our day, experience and witness how they are so little helped by the rich. This neglect of the poor offends the holy angels and grieves the Holy Spirit, since they witness how the dignity of souls are so degraded and abased because of the vile greed for gold. Charitable acts and almsgiving to the poor are acceptable sacrifices to the Lord. More readily acceptable to the Lord, however, are offerings and sacrifices of love, which is represented by the gold offered by the Magi to Christ; continual prayer to God, which is represented by the incense; and the fulfillment of one's work and true mortifications, which is represented by the myrrh. All that we do for the Lord should be offered up to him with fervent affection. In order for one's offerings and sacrifices to be accepted by God, they must be borne out of true and genuine responses to the stimuli of love which we have received from him. Those who use their spiritual graces and temporal wealth properly, who do not have inordinate greed for material wealth and riches, and who do charities to the poor for the sake of Christ gain rewards from God and eternal life.

2. Act of Praise of the Blessed Virgin Mary

Hail Mary, peerless offspring of the omnipotence of the Father, beloved Mother of the wisdom of the Son, and of the enrapturing goodness of the Holy Spirit! Hail Mary, who fills heaven and earth with your gentle light. You have the plenitude of grace, the Lord is with you, even the only-begotten Son of the Father, and the one only Son of the love of your virgin heart, your sweetest child, and your Beloved Lord. Blessed are you among women, for you have annulled the curse of Eve, and has brought back an everlasting blessing. And blessed is the Fruit of your womb, Jesus Christ, the Lord and Creator of all things, who evermore blesses and sanctifies, enriches, and quickens all things. Amen.

O Virgin Mary, I praise you for your most spotless and exceeding purity by which you prepared within your virginal womb a most sacred and sacrosanct sanctuary for your Divine Son. O Compassionate Mary, I praise you for your profound humility by which you merited to be raised high above all the angels and saints. O Loving Mary, I praise you for your ineffable love which unites you inseparably to God. Amen.

V. O ever-Blessed Virgin Mary, Mother of the Incarnate Word.

R. Pray for us who have recourse to you.

Let us pray. I give thanks to you, O God the Eternal Father who, in your divine omnipotence, created the Blessed Virgin Mary, exempted her from original sin, and illumined, sanctified, and blessed her to be the Mother of your only begotten Son, Jesus Christ. Let the power of your majesty and the immensity of your love for her be glorified, praised, and proclaimed for all eternity. I give thanks to you, O God the Eternal Son who, in your divine wisdom, elected the Blessed Virgin Mary to be your Mother, made her to be conceived without sin, assumed her body and soul to heaven, and elevated her as Queen of all creatures. Let all creatures in heaven and on earth, praise and worship you on account of your love for her. I give thanks to you, O God the Eternal Spirit who, in your divine goodness, gave humanity to the Incarnate Word in the womb of the Blessed Virgin Mary, descended as tongues of fire upon her and on the Apostles on Pentecost Day, and enriched her with all the favors and gifts of your powerful right hand. Let the sanctity and equity of your love for her be praised and magnified for all eternity. Through Christ our Lord. Amen.

WEEK 3: THE THIRD SORROW OF THE
BLESSED VIRGIN MARY - THE LOSS OF THE
CHILD JESUS

Each year the parents of Jesus went to Jerusalem
for the feast of Passover, and when he was twelve
years old, they went up as usual for the festival.
When the festival had ended, as they were returning, the boy Jesus stayed behind in Jerusalem, but
his parents did not know it. Thinking that he was
in the caravan, they journeyed for a day. Then
they started to look for him among their relatives
and acquaintances. When they did not find him,
they returned to Jerusalem to look for him.
(Lk. 2:41-45).

**Day 15:   The Journey of the Holy Family for
the Festival in Jerusalem**

**1. The Journey of the Holy Family to Jerusa-
lem for the Festival**

After they had returned from Egypt and set-
tled down in Nazareth, Jesus, Mary, and Joseph
went every year to the Jerusalem temple for the
feast of Passover. Whenever they went to Jerusalem for the feast, they were accompanied, in a
most solemn procession, by tens of thousands of
angels who could be seen only by Jesus, Mary, and
Joseph. The distance between Nazareth and Jerusalem was in the neighborhood of 90 miles or 145
kilometers. The holy angels, according to the

command and disposition of the Incarnate Word, performed musical accompaniments for the Holy Family both in going to and returning from Jerusalem.

As reported by Luke, the Child Jesus was twelve years old when they made this memorable trip to Jerusalem. He desired that they make the journey to Jerusalem on foot. For already the Child Jesus had begun to assume hardships in the service of his Eternal Father and for our salvation. He refused to make use of his immense power for lessening the difficulties of the journey, but undertook it as a man subject to suffering and allowed all the natural effects of walking long distance and of the weather to afflict him. One of such effects was the fatigue and exhaustion caused by long distance travel by foot. He always made the journey on foot. Sometimes, Mary would hold him by the hand and, at other times, Joseph would do so. Joseph and Mary did not interfere with the wishes of Jesus to walk on foot, since they knew of his desire to suffer for the human race.

Many times, when the Child Jesus was fatigued from the journey and from the heat of the sun, his most loving and prudent Mother, Mary, would be moved to the most tender and tearful compassion for him. She would ask him how he was doing and she would wipe his divine countenance with the hem of her veil. She was wont to do this on her knees and with ineffable reverence.

She knew her Son also to be the Son of the Eternal Father and to be true God and true Man. She did not ever fail in the love due him as from a true and natural mother; at the same time, she showed him all the reverence due to him as her God and Creator. The Child Jesus would respond with thanks and speak of the delight with which he accepted these hardships for the glory of the Eternal Father and for the salvation of the human race. Their journey to Jerusalem was made short by these conversations and discussions and by the canticles of divine praises with which the angels accompanied them. From time to time, the wind would flutter through the hair of the Child Jesus as he walked along.

The tunic Jesus wore was made by his Mother, Mary, when they were in Egypt and when Jesus was a year old. When he turned one year old in Egypt, she procured some wool in its natural and uncolored state, knitted it very finely with her own hands and wove a tunic of it. The tunic was made of one piece and without any seam. She wove it upon a small loom, by meshes, crocheting it of one seamless piece in a mysterious manner. The garment was entirely even and uniform, without any seams. Its color was a mixture of brown and silver-gray. She mixed the brown and silver-gray dyes in such perfect quantities that the final color could neither be called brown, nor silver, nor gray, but a mixture of them all. She cut the neck of the tunic evenly round. Through this opening at its neck she wore the tunic over the head of the Infant Jesus. When she wore him the seamless tunic, it fitted him perfectly from his neck to his ankle, although she had taken no measurement of him beforehand. The sleeves extended to slightly before his elbows. This tunic continually grew with him, adjusting itself to his body as he grew. The tunic neither wore out, nor faded, nor lost its newness. It was the same tunic that the executioners took off from him in order to scourge him and afterwards to crucify him.

After they had returned from Egypt to Nazareth, Mary, his Mother, also made him a mantle or cape, which he wore over his shoulders. Like the tunic, it grew with the Lord, was of the same color, only a little darker and was woven in the same way. The garment which the Redeemer of the world laid aside in order to wash the feet of his Apostles was the same mantle or cape that his Mother had made for him. It was also the same cape that the soldiers tore into four parts at his crucifixion; and it was the same tunic that one of them took for himself. "When the soldiers had crucified Jesus, they took his clothes and divided them into four parts, one for each soldier. They also took his tunic; now the tunic was seamless, woven in one piece from the top." (Jn. 19:23).

She also wove him a pair of sandals of strong thread, like hempen shoes, which he wore until he began his public ministry at the age of thirty years old when he took them off and walked barefooted.

During the journey to Jerusalem, Jesus, Mary, and Joseph performed many heroic works of charity and miracles for the benefit of souls. They converted many to the knowledge of the Lord, freed them from their sins and justified them before God, leading them on the way of life eternal. But as it was not yet time for Jesus to manifest himself, all these works were done in secret. They sometimes passed the nights in lodgings, sometimes on open fields, but Mother and Child were never separated or apart from each other. At all times Mary attended upon Jesus, watching his actions in order to imitate and follow them closely. The same thing she did in the temple, where she joined in the prayers and petitions of the Incarnate Word to his Eternal Father. She witnessed and emulated the humble and profound reverence by which Jesus, in his humanity, prayed to the Father.

The holy angels intoned hymns of sweetest harmony in honor of the Incarnate Word when they entered the temple as they did on their journey. Mary and Joseph also saw the angels and heard their angelic melodies; and the holy couple was filled with new light, consolation, and wisdom. Her purest heart blazed up and was inflamed in divine love. The Most High showered upon her new gifts and blessings. By means of these blessings, God was preparing her for the adversities ahead which she was to suffer in union with Jesus Christ. For, many times after these consolations, she saw in several visions all the affronts, ignominies, and sufferings awaiting her most holy Son in that same city of Jerusalem. She shed many tears in anticipation of the injuries to be borne by her sweetest Son and at the thought of the sufferings and the ignominious death to which he was destined. (Is. 53:3). Her soul was filled with anguish also because she herself was to witness all this with her own eyes. But she was also consoled because many souls would be redeemed by the sufferings of her Son.

2. Act of Reparation to the Mother of Sorrows

O Blessed ever-Virgin Mary, Mother of God, I praise and extol the Almighty Father for all that he did for you and for blessing you with his most exalted favors. I also thank Jesus Christ, the Only Begotten Son of God and your Son, for his delightful charity toward you. I adore and thank him for the redemption which he has gained for sinners and for his wonderful bounty toward souls. I give thanks and praise to the Holy Spirit whose power formed the humanity of the Incarnate Word in your womb and by whose power the Incarnate Word exercised his ministry and works.

I weep with sorrow over the stubborn blindness of people in failing to acknowledge the loving protection, which they have in Jesus Christ and in you as a relief from all their troubles and necessities. The Lord spared himself no exertion and left no means of graces unused in order to gain for us the inestimable treasures of heaven. He gave us the secure pledges of his glorious love and procured for us easy and efficacious means to enjoy and apply them for our use and for our eternal salvation. He offers us his protection as well as yours. O most pure Mother of God, you receive with maternal affection all those who fervently and devoutly desire to be your children and the servant of the Lord. By the love which he has given you, you embrace them with open arms, you become their Intercessor and Advocate before your Son, and you manifest toward them your most liberal kindness. Beseech our Lord and Savior, Jesus Christ, to send his light into the hearts of people and to awaken in them the right intention of receiving his message, love, and presence.

O most sorrowful Mother, your heart was wounded and lacerated with grief at the mistreatments, blows, spittle, and injustice suffered by your Son. I make reparation and console you and your Son for his sorrows and yours. By your intercession and by the merits of our Lord Jesus Christ, which he offered to the Eternal Father, may we obtain true sorrow for our sins, avert the chastisement of God, fulfill his will all the days of our life, and obtain eternal life. O Blessed and holy Mary, you alone of all mortals lived according to the will and conduct of your Son, Jesus Christ, without departing in the least from the closest imitation of his life and doctrines. You are most prudent, full of knowledge and wisdom; gain for me eternal love, eternal light, and eternal life. Amen.

Day 16: The Journey of Mary and Joseph Back to Nazareth Without Jesus

1. How the Boy Jesus Stayed Behind in Jerusalem

Every year the parents of Jesus went to Jerusalem for the feast of Passover. When he was twelve years old, they went up as usual for the festival. (Lk. 2:42). This festival of Passover or unleavened Bread lasted seven days; the more solemn days were the first and the last days. The Holy Family remained in Jerusalem during the whole week, spending their time in acts of worship and devotion as the rest of the Jews. However, their worship and devotion was more eminent and pleasing to God than that of the other people. The Blessed Mother and holy Joseph, during these days, received favors and blessings beyond the conception of the human mind.

Having thus spent all the seven days of the feast in Jerusalem, the Holy Family decided to return home to Nazareth. It was customary at that time, on their way home after the festival, for the men to travel separately from the women for the sake of decency and for greater recollection on their journey home. The children who accompanied their parents to Jerusalem could go with either of their parents back home. Jesus knew in his divine fore-knowledge that the scholars of the law and scribes would meet in three days' time in the temple to discuss the coming of the Messiah, and he wanted to remain behind in Jerusalem in order to meet and discuss the matter with them. Thus, knowing that the men would soon separate from the women, and knowing that he was to remain behind in Jerusalem for three days, and knowing that Mary, his Mother, would never let him off from her sight, the Boy Jesus diverted the attention of his Mother away from him by infusing her with contemplative visions of the Most Holy God. Jesus made his mother so caught up in her beatific visions that she was only able to make use of her natural faculties in so far as they were necessary for her to know her way back to Jerusalem. The Boy Jesus also infused Joseph with a most exalted and contemplative visions of God such that Joseph was wrapped in it that he did not realize that the twelve year old Jesus was neither with him nor with his Mother. Having deeply infused Mary and Joseph with visions of God and heaven, the Boy Jesus, without their knowledge, sneaked away from them and hastened through the streets of Jerusalem out of their sight.

Mary was entirely enraptured in the sweetness and consolation of the divine visions that, at first, she failed to notice that Jesus was not with her. When a considerable length of miles had been travelled by her and the other women pilgrims on her caravan, she came out of the vision and found herself without the company of her most holy and beloved Son. She then supposed him to be with Joseph. Although she would never let him out of her sight not only because she loved him dearly but also because she delighted in his company more than any other creature, human or angelic, nonetheless, not seeing the Boy Jesus by her side, she supposed that he had accompanied Joseph so that Joseph would enjoy his company and the sweetest melodies of the angels.

Joseph was also so wrapped in his own contemplative visions of God that, at first, he did not notice that Jesus was not with him. And when he later came out of his visions, he became aware that Jesus was not with him. He supposed that Jesus was with his Mother. Thus, while, on the one hand, Joseph thought that Jesus was with Mary; Mary, on the other hand, thought that Jesus was with Joseph. As such, Mary and Joseph continued on their home journey for an entire day, as Luke tells us, without Jesus.

2. Act of Consolation and Compassion to the Mother of Sorrows

O most loving Mother of my Lord Jesus Christ, behold, I, a poor and pitiable sinner, come to you with deep devotion and contrition. You neither reject nor despise anyone who turns to you with a contrite heart. O Immaculate Heart of Mary, let me obtain mercy from you as so many others sinners have obtained it through your intercession. How is it possible that grace could be refused to anyone who implores it from your Heart of mercy? I beseech you to obtain for me the grace to honor and love you with all my strength. Most tender and compassionate Mother, you know how much my heart is afflicted in compassion for you because the intensity of your sufferings was so great that all mankind together would have been incapable of supporting it. Oh, what unutterable bitterness filled your soul when you contemplated the disfigured form of your beloved Son, when you received his mangled and lifeless Body into your virginal arms, and pressing the Body tenderly to your maternal heart, embraced the sacred Body. You bedewed his sacred Body with a stream of sorrowful tears, and finally rested your agonizing heart on the wounded brow of your Jesus!

I recall, with devotion, your inexpressible anguish; I beseech you to obtain for me the pardon of my sins. O Mary, intercede for me with Jesus, whom you bore in your arms! O Jesus! O Mary, by your unutterable sufferings, have pity on me, a miserable sinner. O dearest Jesus, show to your Heavenly Father all the wounds and anguish which you bore for me! O sweetest Virgin, show him all the tears which you shed for me! O Mother, show him all the agony, all the anguish of heart which you endured for me. O Mary, I beseech you, through this most painful mystery of your dolors, obtain mercy for me from God the Father. Take the mangled and dead Body of your beloved Son into your maternal arms, and offer him to the Eternal Father in the same manner as you once offered to the Eternal Father the pierced Side of Jesus and your own broken heart, the bitter sufferings of Jesus and your painful compassion, his and your burning tears, and his and your sighs; in a word, offer to the Father everything which Jesus and you suffered on earth so that, through these same sufferings, you may obtain mercy and pardon for me, the perfect amendment of my life, and the sanctification and salvation of my soul. Amen.

V. O Sorrowful and Immaculate Heart of Mary.

R. Pray for us who have recourse to you.

Let us pray. O Jesus Christ, Lord of lords and King of kings, you hold power and dominion over all creation, you triumph and reign over your enemies; you are worthy to be worshipped. You are supreme Goodness, pure Holiness, and infinite Power. You have need of none outside yourself and your will governs all created things. There are many things that divert and distract me from rendering you the worship due you, who art my God. There are many dangers besieging the salvation of my soul. Grant that, through the intercession of your most holy Mother, I may keep my mind focused on you, my God and render you the pure worship due you. Who is like you, O King of kings, who dwells on high and who looks upon the humble in heaven and on earth? Who is like you, O Lord of lords, who is Almighty and depends upon no one? Who is like you, O true God and true Man, who humbles the proud, and casts down those whom the blind world calls powerful? Who is like you, O omnipotent God, who alone holds power and dominion over all creation and who triumphs and reigns over his enemies? By the victories and triumphs of your mighty arm, grant me a share in the victories which you have won over evil and a share in your kingdom of love, light, and life forever and ever. Amen.

Day 17: The Whereabouts of the Boy Jesus are Unknown

1. The Boy Jesus Is No Where To Be Found

On their way back from Jerusalem from the festival in Jerusalem to their respective cities and homes, it was customarily at that time for the men and the women to travel separately and for husbands and wives and their young children re-unite at an agreed upon place in their city of domicile. As the Jerusalem pilgrims continued on their journey back to their respective homes, they gradually thinned out and re-united with other family members at their mutually agreed upon places. Thus, before they began their separate journeys back to Nazareth, Mary and Joseph had agreed at the place where they would re-unite before continuing their journey together, with Jesus, back to their house. The left Jerusalem in the morning, and after a day's journey, Mary and Joseph, at last, met at the mustering place that was previously agreed upon by both of them. They met at the mustering place on the evening after leaving Jerusalem. When they met at the place, Mary realized that the Boy Jesus was not with Joseph and Joseph also realized that Jesus was not with Mary either. When they discovered that Jesus was not with either of them, the two of them stood still and were speechless for a few minutes. After sometime, they somewhat recovered from their shock regarding the fact that Jesus was not with either of them. They then thought that he was with one of their relatives or friends. But even if he was with relatives or friends, they said to themselves, how did Jesus elude their vigilance? The three of them, Jesus, Mary, and Joseph had always been together in Jerusalem; so, how, when, and where did Jesus, they asked themselves, take leave of them to go and be with relatives and friends?

Mary blamed and reproached herself for letting Jesus out of her sight. Joseph, on his part, blamed and reproached himself for failing in his God-given mission to watch over Jesus on earth. They then took counsel with each other as to what was to be done in order to locate Jesus. Neither of them had any suspicion that Jesus had remained behind in Jerusalem and that this was all the Lord's doing.

Jesus did not tell Mary and Joseph that he was staying behind in Jerusalem to meet with the scholars and teachers of the law in three days' time because if he had told them, then Mary and Joseph would have decided to stay behind with him. And if the Holy Family had decided to stay behind in Jerusalem for three extra days, then their relatives and friends from Nazareth who also came to Jerusalem for the festival would have wanted to know why. In addition, if Jesus had told them that he wanted to stay behind in Jerusalem for three days in order to have a meeting with the biblical scholars, his relatives and friends would have responded that if he wanted to listen to the scholars of the scriptures in Jerusalem and ask them questions, then he should ask they themselves, his relatives and friends, the questions he wanted to ask those scholars in Jerusalem or that when he got back to Nazareth, he should go and consult the biblical scholars in Nazareth.

And Jesus did not also disclose his plan to stay behind in Jerusalem for a few days to Mary and Joseph because it was unthinkable, from the human perspective, that they would leave him behind in Jerusalem. And if Mary and Joseph had left the twelve-year old Jesus behind in Jerusalem, then their relatives and friends who came with them from Nazareth to Jerusalem for the festival would have questioned why his parents were leaving the twelve-year old Boy Jesus, whose identity as the Messiah had not yet been disclosed to them, behind in Jerusalem. In addition, if Jesus and Mary had returned to Nazareth without Jesus, then their relatives and friends in Nazareth who did not go for the festival would also have started asking questions. Thus, given the complexity of the situation and given that it was not yet time for the revelation of his identity as the Messiah, Jesus, in his divine wisdom, decided to conceal his intention and plan from everyone, including Mary and Joseph.

2. Intercessory Prayer to Our Lady of Sorrows for Married Couples

O Holy Mary, Mother of God, afflicted with sorrows and sufferings in defense of your marriage and of your family, with you I praise and give thanks to the Incarnate Word, Jesus Christ, your Son, who established the sacrament of holy matrimony to sanctify the natural union of man and wife for the good of the spouses and for the propagation of the human race. Protect married couples from the wiles and snares of the enemy, enrich and adorn them with your merits and protection, with spousal unity and fidelity, and with love and respect for one another. I pray also for those married persons in my family, church, circle of friends, office, ministry, or business who are going through grave marital difficulties; look with pity upon them and beseech your Son, Jesus Christ, so that the manipulations and machinations of the enemies of Christ may be foiled and so that the will of God may prevail and be established. May the reign and peace of Christ be established in every family and home, especially in those whom I know and in those who seek your intercession and who invoke the holy name of Jesus Christ. Amen.

V. Sorrowful and Immaculate Heart of Mary.

R. Pray for us who have recourse to you.

Let us pray. O good and gentle Holy Spirit, bounteous Giver of all graces, most gracious Paraclete, I implore you, through the glorious death of Jesus on the cross and the intercession of his Blessed Mother, to preserve and bless more abundantly all married couples who are in holy matrimony and to save all troubled marriages. Grant them your cleansing power, enlighten and adorn them with all the virtues and graces necessary for them to preserve and keep sanctified their marriages, and enable them to remain steadfast and persevere unto the end. Who with the Father and the Son lives and reigns forever and ever. Amen.

Day 18: The Search for the Missing Boy Jesus

1. The Search for the Missing Boy Jesus

Mary and Joseph began their search for the Boy Jesus by, first of all, asking their relatives and friends whether he was with any of them. (Lk. 2:44). If the response from their friends and relatives was negative, they would then ask them whether they could provide any information concerning the whereabouts of Jesus. None of their relatives and friends had as much as seen Jesus from the time of their departure from Jerusalem. This lack of information only served to increase the anxiety of Mary and Joseph. When Mary and Joseph had asked all their relatives and friends who went with them to Jerusalem for the festival regarding the whereabouts of Jesus and when none of them responded that they had seen Jesus and had no information as to his whereabouts, the afflicted Mother then turned in prayer to her holy guardian angels to tell her the location of her Son. She prayed to them, saying: My angelic friends and guardian angels, you well know the cause of my sorrow. In this bitter affliction, be my consolation and give me the information regarding the whereabouts of my Beloved Son so that I may seek and find him. Give some relief to my wounded heart, which is torn from its happiness and life so that I may know where to find him.

Although the holy angels, who cannot lose sight of our Redeemer, knew of his whereabouts, nonetheless, they have been commanded by the Most Holy Trinity to conceal the whereabouts of the Incarnate Word from Mary and Joseph. The Three Persons of the Blessed Trinity wished to use this occasion to furnish Mary and Joseph with great merits. In addition, the reason why Jesus stayed behind in Jerusalem had not yet been fulfilled and, therefore, it was not yet time to reveal the secret of the whereabouts of Jesus to Mary and Joseph. The angels, thus, responded by speaking words of consolation to her without manifesting to her the whereabouts and the doings of the God-Man. They, however, assured her that she would soon find her Son. This evasive answer of the holy angels only served to raise to new heights the anxiety and worries of Mary and Joseph. This increased anxiety caused Mary to break out in tears of inmost grief. Unlike the woman in the Gospel of Luke who was in search of a mere missing drachma (Lk. 15:8–10), Mary was in search of her missing Child.

Having failed to locate her Son among her relatives and friends and the angels, having failed to provide her with information regarding the whereabouts of Jesus, Mary began discussing within herself the different possibilities regarding where her Son might be. The first thought that presented itself to her mind was that Archelaus who had succeeded Herod his father in the government of Judea (Mt. 2:22) may have taken the Boy Jesus prisoner. For Archelaus, who had infiltrated everywhere with his spies, might have received report about the presence of Jesus in Jerusalem and might have sent soldiers to the Boy Jesus and they might have taken him prisoner. Although she knew from Holy Scriptures and from her conversations with her most holy Son and Teacher that the time for his Passion and Death had not yet come and that Archelaus would not take away the life of Jesus, nonetheless, she was filled with dread at the thought that they could have taken him prisoner and might have begun to maltreat him. She also knew that her Son, though God of heaven and earth, would not resist the mistreatments and torture that Archelaus might inflict on him. However, having ascertained from her holy guardian angels that Archelaus had not taken Jesus prisoner, she felt somewhat relieved; at the same time, however, her worries about the whereabouts of her missing Child neither abated nor ceased.

Next, she considered whether her Child, Jesus, might have decided to take up abode in the desert with his precursor, John the Baptist. Then she prayed to her Son, Jesus, saying: O Lord God of my soul! You are impelled by your desire of suffering for people and by your immense love to avoid no labor or pain; but on the contrary, I fear, O my Lord and God, that you seek it on purpose. Where shall I go and where shall I find you? Do you wish to deprive me of life by the sword of severance from your presence? Why, O my Lord, have you enriched me with the delights of your infancy, if I am so soon to lose the grace of your loving presence? If the privilege of being your Mother can be of any avail in finding you, my God and my highest Good, do help me find you. But am I not worthy of your clemency, since my eyes can find no traces of you? Do, O Lord, permit it, and make me worthy of finding you so that I may go with you in the desert, to sufferings, labors, tribulations, or whatever you will. My Lord, my soul desires to merit at least in part to share your sorrows and torments and to live in your service and presence. Amen.

Believing that her most holy Son was with John the Baptist in the desert, she decided to go and meet them there. She had made up her mind to go to the desert in search of her Son when her holy guardian angels strongly urged her not to undertake the journey, since the Incarnate Word was not there. However, they would not give her any clue as to where she might find Jesus.

Next, she considered whether Jesus had gone to Bethlehem, his birth place, to the Cave of the Nativity. She then made up her mind to go to Bethlehem in the hope of finding him in the Cave of the Nativity. However, her holy guardian angels likewise prevented her from going to Bethlehem; they told her that he was not so far away. The Blessed Mother heard these answers and properly discerned that although the holy angels knew the whereabouts of Jesus, they had been commanded by the Lord to withhold the information from her so that he could accomplish the purpose for which he had placed himself out of her sight and that of Joseph but not out of their mind.

Having humanly exhausted all possibilities as to where she might find Jesus and her guardian angels, under the command of God, having refused to give her any information as to the whereabouts of Jesus, she began weeping profusely again.

The Gospel of Luke tells us that when they did not find Jesus, they went back to Jerusalem to look for him. (Lk. 2:45). Mary and Joseph walked that evening and all through the night back to Jerusalem. On the morning of the first day that Jesus was missing, Mary and Joseph walked through the streets of Jerusalem, asking different people whether they had seen a missing twelve-year old Boy, their Son. The answer they got from people was always in the negative. On the second day, they continued their search for the missing Jesus and they could not find him either. On the third day, Mary and Joseph continued their search for the missing Jesus; at this time, her anxieties and tears were understandably without abatement or cessation. She neither slept nor ate anything for three whole days. She searched the highways and byways of Jerusalem. She sought him with due diligence and wisdom for three whole days without any positive result.

On the third day that Jesus went missing, she had the first breakthrough. Some of the women whom she had asked whether they had seen her Son asked Mary to describe him. And Mary answered thus: My Beloved Son is radiant, ruddy, and outstanding among tens of thousands of people. One of the women, hearing Mary thus describe Jesus, said to her: This Child, with those same characteristics, came yesterday to my door to ask for alms, and I gave some to him. His grace and good looks ravished my heart. And when I gave him alms, I felt myself overcome by compassion, emotions, and tears to see a Child so gracious in poverty and adorable begging for alms.

This was the first good news in three days that the sorrowful Mother had heard about her Only Beloved Son. A little elated, she continued in her quest for the missing Jesus. She met other persons who also spoke of him in like manner. Guided by the information available to her, she directed her steps to the hospital in the city, since she knew that part of his mission on earth was also to cure the sick. She also knew that if her Son was hungry, he would not need to beg for food since he could, if he wanted to do so, work miracles of food to satisfy his hunger. When she got to the hospital and inquired about him there, she was informed that a Child of that description had visited the sick in the hospital, had given them some alms, and had spoken words of consolation and healing to the sick.

The report of these doings of her Beloved Son caused sentiments of sweetest and most tender affection in her heart. While she was in the hospital premises, the thought suddenly struck her from on high that since he was neither with the poor on the streets nor with the sick in the hospital; he was certainly in the temple, the house of God and the house of prayer. The holy angels encouraged her to hasten up her steps to the temple for her Son was certainly in the precincts of the temple. They said to her: O Lady and our Queen, the hour of your consolation is at hand; soon you will see the Light of your eyes; hasten your footsteps and go to the temple.

On his part, the glorious patriarch, Joseph, had agreed with Mary that they should go to different directions in the city in the hope of increasing their chances of finding Jesus. During these three days they were in search of Jesus, he too had suffered

unimaginable sorrows and afflictions. He had neither rested, nor slept, nor ate, nor drank for the
three days. In fact, he was in serious danger of losing his life during this time if the hand of the Lord
had not preserved his life and if Mary, his spouse,
had not consoled him and compelled him to take
some food and rest. At the moment it dawn on
Mary that Jesus was in the temple, especially after
her holy guardian angels had also confirmed it,
Joseph, also based on the information he had received from various people in the city, came to the
hospital and met Mary within the vicinity of the
hospital. The Lord God had synchronized their
movements such that they both met in the hospital
facilities. The guardian angel of Joseph then told
him to proceed to the temple where he would find
Jesus. Following the advice of their holy guardian
angels, the most pure Mary and Joseph betook
themselves as fast as they could to the temple.

2. Special Intention Prayer to Mary Mother of Sorrows

O Blessed ever-Virgin Mary, Mother of God,
Queen of heaven and earth, I acknowledge you as
my Mother and Queen. With Jesus our Lord, I exult and glorify God the Father for you. You are the
treasurer and dispenser of all the graces in heaven
and on earth. Whatever you ordain and dispose
for us, who are heirs of God and co-heirs with
Christ, is confirmed by the Most Blessed Trinity.

And whatever you ask for us from the Most Holy Trinity is conceded to you. I invoke your divine assistance for the following blessings.

(*state your intentions here*).

O Holy Mary, Mother of God, afflicted with sorrows and sufferings, through your intercession and the favor of the Eternal Father, may I be granted the privilege of remaining constantly close to our Savior, Jesus Christ. Grant me abhorrence for sin, the perfect amendment of my life, and the grace to grow in the practice of virtues. O Mother and Queen of virtues! O Mother of the immortal King of ages! Free me from spiritual lukewarmness and gross negligence. And through your clemency make me a partaker of your special favors and graces. Amen.

O Blessed Virgin Mary, Mother of Light and Queen of Peace, beseech the Holy Spirit to preserve, prosper, and protect me and to assist me by his grace to be faithful to Christ. Amen.

O Mother of God, you are most blessed among all women, Mother most prudent, strong, and constant, unconquered by any fault, unfailing in your service, and most faithful in your love toward your Son, Jesus Christ. Grant that I may be enlightened anew in order to better love, honor, and appreciate you, the greatest creature of the Most Holy Trinity and to love more profoundly Jesus Christ our Savior, who is our Lord forever and ever. Amen.

V. Pray for us, O most sorrowful Virgin.

R. That we may be made worthy of the promises of Christ.

Let us pray. O Most Loving Lord Jesus, I thank you with humble and loving affection for all the blessings that I have received in abundance from you. The memory of your blessings is stored in me, and especially memorable to me are that you have entrusted me to the care and solicitude of your Blessed Mother, that you have redeemed me from the kingdom of darkness and transferred me to your Kingdom, which is a Kingdom of light, life, and love and of justice, peace, and joy in the Holy Spirit. I also thank you that you have called me to follow you, that you have drawn me closer to you, that you have dissembled and excused my sins and faults, and that you have added thereto many favors to me. O Lord Jesus, I thank you for all the blessings which you have wrought for me and for the whole human race. Amen.

Day 19: The Boy Jesus in the Temple

1. The Meeting of the Boy Jesus with Scripture Scholars in the Temple

When the Boy Jesus sneaked away from his parents, he knew that the scholars of the Jewish law in Jerusalem would be meeting in the temple in three days' time. He also knew that it was part of the divine plan for him to remain in Jerusalem as a twelve year old boy for three days. Foreseeing in his divine fore-knowledge all that was to happen, he offered it up to his Eternal Father for the benefit of souls. During those three days he begged for alms not because he needed to do so but in order to show us the importance and virtue of almsgiving and so that he would use the opportunity of the alms he would receive from people to bless those who would give them to him. During the three days that Mary and Joseph could not locate him, Jesus also visited the hospitals, consoling the sick therein and gave them the alms that he had collected. He enlightened them interiorly and led them back to the way of salvation. He secretly restored them to bodily and spiritual health. Of those who gave him alms, he performed wonders and miracles for them and gave them a great abundance of grace and enlightenment.

On the third day that he was absent from Mary and Joseph, the rabbis and scholars of the law met in a certain part of the temple in order to confer among themselves about some doubts concerning the coming of the Messiah. The report of the visions of angels to the shepherds, the visits of the Magi, and the prophecy of Simeon, had spread around and about and had become well-known that the word on the street was either that the coming of the Messiah was imminent or that he was already in the world.

The rabbis and scholars of the law were all seated in their places puffed-up with the authority customary to those who are teachers and who are considered or who consider themselves to be learned. The Boy Jesus came to the meeting of these learned and distinguished men. He is the King of kings, and the Lord of lords (Rev. 19: 16). He is infinite Wisdom. (I Cor. 1:24). He who is the Messiah presented himself before these teachers as a humble student, and told them that he had come to hear their discussion, disputation, and doubt. The doubt was: whether the Messiah had already come into the world; if the response to this question is negative, whether it is known when and how he would come into the world.

The scholars of the law began to discuss the topic of the day, and their opinions on the matter were much at variance. Majority of them maintained that the Messiah had not yet come into the world, and when he would do so, he would come with great power, might, and authority and he would, by the exercise of his great power, overthrow the Romans and establish a political kingdom for the Hebrew nation. They argued that as yet there was no one in the nation who had such power and there was no hope of throwing off the yoke of the Romans. They believed that the redemption and kingdom to be established by the Christ would be an earthly one. A few of them, however, argued and, indeed, believed that the glory, the majesty, and the power of the Redeemer, and the redemption that he is to bring to the world would not be of an earthly kind, but that it would be heavenly, spiritual, and eternal and that the redemption is not intended for only the nation of Israel, but also for everyone in all nations.

The Teacher of truth, Jesus, foresaw that the discussion would end with the common error of the majority of the scholars and teachers prevailing over the correct opinion of the minority of the scholars and teachers. The few who held the correct opinion had been silenced by the authoritative, sophistical, blind, and erroneous arguments of the majority. Inasmuch as the Lord had come into the world in order to give testimony of the truth (Jn. 18:37), which he is himself, he was not going to let prevail the manifest, common, and invincible error about his coming and mission. Therefore, the Teacher of teachers, Jesus, stepped into their midst with great majesty and grace and by his pleasing appearance he awakened in the hearts of these learned men a desire to listen attentively to him.

The twelve-year old Jesus then spoke to the learned men and rabbis. He said that he has heard their disputations, and he completely understood the debate regarding the coming of the Messiah and the answers given to it. The Prophets say that the coming of the Messiah shall be in great power and majesty. For example, Isaiah says that the

Messiah shall be our Law-giver and King, and shall save his people (Isa. 30:27); David that the Messiah shall crush all his enemies (Ps. 94:3); Daniel that all tribes and nations shall serve him (Dan. 7:14); and Ecclesiasticus that he shall come with a great multitude of the saints (Eccl. 24:3). All the other prophets and scriptures testify to similar promises.

He continued that, however, the doubt regarding the nature of the coming of the Messiah arises from the comparison of the foregoing scriptural passages with other passages by the Prophets. For example, the same Isaiah says that the Messiah grew up like a young plant, and like a root out of dry ground; he had no form or majesty that we should look at him, and no beauty that we should desire him. He was despised and rejected by men, a man of sorrows and acquainted with grief; and as one from whom men hide their faces he was despised, and we esteemed him not. He has borne our griefs and carried our sorrows; yet we esteemed him stricken, smitten by God, and afflicted. He was wounded for our transgressions; he was crushed for our iniquities; upon him was the chastisement that made us whole, and by his wounds we are healed. All we like sheep have gone astray; and the Lord has laid on him the iniquity of us all. He was oppressed and afflicted, yet he opened not his mouth; like a lamb that is led to the slaughter, like a sheep that before its shearers is silent, he opened not his mouth. By oppression and judgment he was taken away; and as for his generation, he was considered cut off out of the land of the living, stricken for the transgression of my people. And they made his grave with the wicked and with a rich man in his death, although he had done no violence, and there was no deceit in his mouth. Yet it was the will of the Lord to crush him, to put him to grief, to make his soul an offering for guilt. (Isa. 53:2-10).

On his part, Jeremiah states that the enemies of the Messiah shall join hands to persecute the Messiah and mix poison with his bread, and they shall attempt to wipe out his name from the earth, although they shall not prevail. (Jer. 11:19). David says that the Messiah shall be the reproach of the people, and shall be trodden under foot and shall be despised as a worm (Ps. 21:78); Zechariah, that he shall come gentle and humble seated upon an insignificant beast (Zech. 9:9). All the Prophets say the same concerning the signs of the promised Messiah.

Therefore, asked the gentle and humble Jesus, how will it be possible to reconcile these two seemly contradictory prophecies? For on the one hand, the ancient prophecies state that the Messiah is to come with the power and majesty of arms in order to conquer kings and monarchs by violence and bloodshed; and, on the other hand, that the Messiah shall come with gentleness and humility. We cannot fail to see that he is to come twice; once to redeem the world and a second time to judge it; the prophecies must be applied to both comings, which gives each school of thoughts regarding the coming of the Messiah its right explanation. And inasmuch as the purpose for each coming is different so must also the conditions must be different.

In his first advent, the Messiah is to come and overthrow the kingdom of the demon and hurl him from his sovereignty over souls. And, therefore, the Messiah must first render satisfaction to God for the whole human race; teach people, by his word and example, the way of eternal life, the way to overcome their enemies, the way to serve and adore their God and Redeemer; and the way to respond to his graces and use well the blessings the Lord bestows on people. All these requirements the Messiah must fulfill in the first coming. In this, his first coming is for the redemption of the human race from the kingdom of darkness to the kingdom of light.

The second coming of the Messiah is for the purpose of exacting an account from all peoples in the general judgment of the world, of giving to each one the reward, good or bad, for his or her works, chastising his enemies in his wrath and indignation. This is what the Prophets say and mean regarding his second coming. Accordingly, when we wish to understand how, as David says, that the Messiah shall reign from sea to sea and how, as said by the other Prophets, that in his advent the Messiah shall be glorious, we cannot interpret all these as referring to visible and terrestrial sovereignty, with all its outward show of pomp and pageantry; but of a spiritual reign in a new Church, which would be extended over all the earth with sovereign power amidst graces and virtues.

Furthermore, the Boy Teacher said that the people of the Hebrew nation, who are under the dominion of the Romans, are in no condition to restore the sovereignty of their nation. However, the inability of the Hebrew nation to overthrow the Romans cannot be held as a proof that the Messiah had not yet come. On the contrary, there are infallible signs that he has already come into the world. For the patriarch Jacob pointed out to his posterity that the scepter will not depart from Judah, nor the mace from between his feet, until he to whom it belongs shall come and the nations shall obey him. (Gen. 49:10). The same is also proved by the words of Daniel that there is an anointed ruler. (Dan. 9:25).

The Child Jesus also said that those of them who wish can remember that a few years ago a light was seen in Bethlehem at midnight, that some poor shepherds saw angels who told them of the birth of the Messiah, that soon afterwards some Kings from the East came guided by a star, seeking the King of the Jews in order to adore him, and that Herod, the father of Archelaus, believing it an established fact that the Messiah has been born, took away the life of so many children, hoping thereby to destroy the new-born Messiah, whom he feared as his rival in the government of Israel. All these were prophesied, and have been fulfilled. The Divine Teacher then concluded by telling them that the Messiah has already come into the world.

The scribes and learned men who heard him speak were all dumbfounded. The interpretation the whole Scriptures by Jesus himself became clear as crystal to the scholars of the law as to the two-fold coming of the Christ. And convinced by his arguments they looked at each other and in great astonishment asked: What miracle is this? What prodigy of a Boy! Where did he come from? Who is this Child? From where and from whom did he get all this learning? Although they were astonished at his prodigy and knowledge, they neither suspected nor thought that the One who had taught them is the Messiah himself. These doctors did not recognize him as the Messiah because they were inflated and arrogant in their own knowledge. Their intellect was obscured by the darkness of their pride such that they could not perceive the divine light shining forth in such profound splendor from him to their intellect. If they had had the humble and loving desire of knowing the truth, his reasoning and presence would have sufficiently convinced them of his identity as the Messiah. However, on account of their blind ignorance and pride, they did not recognize that Jesus, the much-expected Messiah, was right there and then in their midst.

2. Act of Compassion to the Sorrowful Mother

1. O Blessed Virgin Mary, Most Loving Mother, in union with that true and faithful filial love which Jesus Christ, in his most glorious and adorable Heart, showed you with perfection on earth and will forever show you in heaven, I offer you my compassion for the sword of sorrow that pierced your Immaculate Heart when Simeon prophesied that a sword shall pierce your soul. By the merits of this sorrow, obtain for me true repentance of my sins, the remission of all my sins, the expiation of all the punishments due to my sins, and the perfect amendment of my life. You are my Advocate before the throne of your Son; turn on me those pitying eyes of yours and grant me your maternal strength and solicitude now and forever. Amen.
Say 1 Hail Mary.

2. O Blessed Virgin Mary, Most Holy Mother, in union with that true and faithful filial love

which Jesus Christ, in his most glorious and adorable Heart, showed you with perfection on earth and will forever show you in heaven, I offer you my compassion for the sword of sorrow that pierced your Immaculate Heart when you were told that Herod was in search of your child to destroy him and you had to flee with the Infant Jesus and Joseph to Egypt. By the merits of this sorrow, obtain for me strength and protection in all my tribulations, especially at the hour of my death. You are my Advocate before the throne of your Son; turn on me those pitying eyes of yours and grant me your maternal peace and prosperity now and forever. Amen.

Say 1 Hail Mary.

3. O Blessed Virgin Mary, Most Sacred Mother, in union with that true and faithful filial love which Jesus Christ, in his most glorious and adorable Heart, showed you with perfection on earth and will forever show you in heaven, I offer you my compassion for the sword of sorrow that pierced your Immaculate Heart when you realized that your Son was missing and for your tears of joy when at last, on the third day, you found him in the temple. By the merits of this sorrow, obtain for me the remembrance of the Passion of Christ and the reward of heaven. You are my Advocate before the throne of your Son; turn on me those

pitying eyes of yours and grant me your maternal graces and gifts now and forever. Amen.
Say 1 Hail Mary.

4. O Blessed Virgin Mary, Most Afflicted Mother, in union with that true and faithful filial love which Jesus Christ, in his most glorious and adorable Heart, showed you with perfection on earth and will forever show you in heaven, I offer you my compassion for the sword of sorrow that pierced your Immaculate Heart when you saw Jesus in extreme anguish and pain as he carried his heavy cross to Calvary. By the merits of this sorrow, obtain for me the perfect practice of all the virtues that are in accordance with my chosen vocation. You are my Advocate before the throne of your Son; turn on me those pitying eyes of yours and grant me your maternal affections and assistance now and forever. Amen.
Say 1 Hail Mary.

5. O Blessed Virgin Mary, Most Sorrowful Mother, in union with that true and faithful filial love which Jesus Christ, in his most glorious and adorable Heart, showed you with perfection on earth and will forever show you in heaven, I offer you my compassion for the sword of sorrow that pierced your Immaculate Heart when Jesus was nailed to the cross and when, after three hours of agony on cross, he bowed his Head and died. By

the merits of this sorrow, obtain for me peace in my family and enlightenment about divine mysteries. You are my Advocate before the throne of your Son; turn on me those pitying eyes of yours and grant me your maternal care and calmness now and forever. Amen.

Say 1 Hail Mary.

6. O Blessed Virgin Mary, Most Faithful Mother, in union with that true and faithful filial love which Jesus Christ, in his most glorious and adorable Heart, showed you with perfection on earth and will forever show you in heaven, I offer you my compassion for the sword of sorrow that pierced your Immaculate Heart when the sacred Side of Jesus was pierced with a lance and when his sacred Body was taken down from the cross and placed on your arms. By the merits of this sorrow, obtain for me consolations in my pains, divine assistance in my work, and the sanctification of my soul. You are my Advocate before the throne of your Son; turn on me those pitying eyes of yours and grant me your maternal blessings and benevolence now and forever. Amen.

Say 1 Hail Mary.

7. O Blessed Virgin Mary, Most Affectionate Mother, in union with that true and faithful filial love which Jesus Christ, in his most glorious and adorable heart, showed you with perfection on

earth and will forever show you in heaven, I offer you my compassion for the sword of sorrow that pierced your Immaculate Heart when the sacred Body of Jesus was laid in the sepulcher. By the merits of this sorrow, obtain for me strength and victory in my spiritual battles with the infernal enemy and your protection at every instance of my life, especially at the moment of my death so that I may see your most radiant and most beautiful face. Obtain for me also from your divine Son the grace to help propagate the devotion to your seven sorrows and the grace to be taken directly from this earthly life to eternal happiness so that your Son, our Lord, Jesus Christ, will be my eternal consolation and joy. You are my Advocate before the throne of your Son; turn on me those pitying eyes of yours and grant me your maternal compassion and consolation now and forever. Amen.

Say 1 Hail Mary.

O Blessed Virgin Mary, I offer you these acts of compassion through the Sacred Heart of Jesus so that they may be cleansed and perfected therein and so that they may be pleasing and acceptable to you. Amen.

O Beloved Mother of God, I offer you the Sacred Heart of Jesus, which abounds in all beatitude. I offer you all the Divine affections by which he predestined, created, and sanctified you from all eternity to be his Mother with the same love and tenderness which he manifested to you on earth, when you carried him in your bosom and nourished him with your milk, and with the same fidelity with which he subjected himself to you, as a Son to a Mother. I offer you the glory and honor to which he elevated you on the day of your Assumption into heaven, when you were exalted high above the choirs of angels and the saints, and proclaimed Queen of heaven and earth. I offer you all these tokens of his love, as if he has presented them to you anew so that you may overlook all my sins and faults and assist me, with all the tenderness of a Mother, now and at all times, especially at the hour of my death so that I may obtain eternal salvation. Amen.

O Blessed Virgin Mary; bless me with your Holy Child, Jesus, now and forever. Amen.

Day 20: The Finding of the Boy Jesus in the Temple

1. Jesus is Found in the Temple

The rabbis and scholars of the law asked Jesus a few questions, which he answered. As he was answering the last question, Mary and Joseph arrived just in time to hear him. The moment Mary and Joseph saw him, all their anguish and sorrows vanished like thin air from their hearts and were replaced by gushes of indescribable joy. When he had finished answering all their questions, all the teachers and scholars of the law arose with stupendous amazement and gave him a standing ovation. Everyone who heard him was amazed at his intelligence and answers. The rabbis and scholars of the law then congratulated Mary and Joseph on their exceptionally brilliant, extraordinarily dignified, and exceedingly majestic Son.

After the learned men had departed and Jesus, Mary, and Joseph were left alone in the temple, Mary said to Jesus, "Son, why have you done this to us? Your father and I have been anxiously searching for you." And he said to them: "Why were you searching for me? Did you not know I had to be in my Father's house?" But they did not understand what he was saying to them. Then he went down to Nazareth with them and was obedient to them. But his Mother treasured all these things in her heart. And Jesus grew in wisdom and stature, and in favor with God and man. (Lk. 2:47-52).

The Evangelist says that neither Mary nor Joseph understood the mystery of the words of Jesus to them. (Lk. 2:50). The reasons the Evangelist said Mary and Joseph did not understand Jesus's statement are because Mary and Joseph were overjoyed at having at last found the Boy Jesus, which was all that mattered for them at that time and because Mary and Joseph had not yet known of the doings of the Boy Jesus for the past three days and what he had just discussed with the scholars of the law. At that time, all that mattered to Mary and

Joseph was that the Boy Jesus who was lost had been found. Having found her missing Child, the Blessed Mother hugged the Child Jesus with maternal affection and lovely tears of joy.

2. Act of Commemoration of the Joys of the Blessed Virgin Mary

1. I rejoice with you, O Blessed Virgin Mary, for all the joys, graces, and merits which are yours in Paradise where all the hierarchies of the angels and all the company of the saints honor, praise, and acknowledge you as the Immaculate Conception.
Say 1 Hail Mary.

2. I rejoice with you, O Chaste Virgin Mary, for all the joys, graces, and merits which are yours in Paradise where all the hierarchies of the angels and all the company of the saints honor, praise, and acknowledge you as the Mother of the Redeemer.
Say 1 Hail Mary.

3. I rejoice with you, O Prudent Virgin Mary, for all the joys, graces, and merits which are yours in Paradise where all the hierarchies of the angels and all the company of the saints honor, praise, and acknowledge you as the Queen of Heaven and Earth.
Say 1 Hail Mary.

4. I rejoice with you, O Holy Virgin Mary, for all the joys, graces, and merits which are yours in Paradise where all the hierarchies of the angels and all the company of the saints honor, praise, and acknowledge you as the Mother of the Church.

Say 1 Hail Mary.

5. I rejoice with you, O Sacred Virgin Mary, for all the joys, graces, and merits which are yours in Paradise where all the hierarchies of the angels and all the company of the saints honor, praise, and acknowledge you as the White Lily of Heaven.

Say 1 Hail Mary.

6. I rejoice with you, O Faithful Virgin Mary, for all the joys, graces, and merits which are yours in Paradise where all the hierarchies of the angels and all the company of the saints honor, praise, and acknowledge you as the Crowning Joy of Heaven.

Say 1 Hail Mary.

7. I rejoice with you, O Loving Virgin Mary, for all the joys, graces, and merits which are yours in Paradise where all the hierarchies of the angels and all the company of the saints honor, praise, and acknowledge you as the Most Blessed of Women.

Say 1 Hail Mary.

Hail Mary, Priceless Pearl of Heaven! Hail Mary, White Lily of the glorious and ever-serene Trinity! Hail Mary, Radiant Rose of heavenly fragrance! Of you the King of heaven was born, and by your milk he was nourished! Nourish my soul with effusions of divine grace, and uphold and succor me, a miserable sinner, now and at the hour of my death. Amen.

O Sacred Virgin Mary, may my praise be accepted by you; give me strength against your enemies now and forever. Amen.

Day 21: Meditations

1. Be Faithful to God in Good and in Bad Times

1. All of the sorrows suffered by the martyrs can never reach the height and depth of the sorrows suffered by the Blessed Virgin Mary. The patience, resignation, and tolerance of Mary can never be equaled by anyone else's. Her love and appreciation of Jesus exceed all that can be shown by any other creature to Jesus. During the three days in which the Child Jesus was lost, God withdrew her supernatural faculties of seeing visions so that she had to rely on her natural faculties to find Jesus. But, in spite of her grave sorrow and affliction, she did not entertain any thought of anger or

indignation, as is so common in other people who allow their passions and faculties to be worked up, even in small matters! Although the sword of sorrow of her missing Child pierced her Immaculate Heart, she continued in the reverence and praise of the Lord and prayed that her most holy Son would be found. But although she was hopeful she would find him, in her great love for him, the uncertainty as to the cause of his staying behind in Jerusalem gave her sleepless nights until she found him. The dread of losing Jesus through our sins should be so great that neither tribulation, nor trouble, nor necessity, nor danger, nor persecution, nor the sword, neither height nor depth should ever withhold us from holding unto our God (Rm. 8:35). If we are faithful to him and if we do not wish to lose him, neither the angels, nor the principalities, nor the powers, nor any other creature can ever deprive us of him.

2. God makes us feel his absence in our life for the purpose of strengthening our faith in him and as chastisement for our sins. The Lord chastises those whom he loves. (Heb. 12:6). During our mortal existence the just and the wicked commonly share the same good and evil lot. However, while the just repent of their sins and faults, the impious harden their hearts in their malice and false security, seeing that the same mishaps befall both themselves and the just, and that no one can tell with moral certainty those who are the friends or ene-

mies of God. But if people would dispassionately and without deceit appeal to their conscience, it would answer each one truthfully regarding what he or she should know. Then you will know the truth, and the truth will set you free. (Jn. 8:32).

3. The gate that leads to life is narrow, and the road is hard, and they who find it are few. (Mt. 7:14). This statement of Jesus means that the spiritual journey that leads from mortal life to eternal life is long, painful, and dangerous. It is long because it is a lifetime journey; it is painful because of the many hardships, tears, trials, tribulations, and sorrows involved; and it is dangerous because human nature is fragile and the enemies of our salvation are astute. Strive to please the Lord Jesus, who suffers ingratitude from so many people and who yet still preserves them in existence and continues to shower his favors on them. Consider his invincible love toward us and how Mary imitated him. Perform acts of kindness, do penance, make sacrifices, observe your pious devotions and spiritual exercises, and pray to the Eternal Father for the salvation of souls. We are to undertake for the love of God the works that God imposes upon us. He rewards those who oblige him.

2. Act of Praise of the Blessed Virgin Mary

Hail Mary, I greet you in union with that reverence with which God the Father greeted you, and by his omnipotence delivered you from every woe and vile of sin. Hail Mary, I greet you in union with that love with which the Son of God enlightened you with his wisdom, and made you a softly shining star, lighting up heaven and earth. Hail Mary, I greet you in union with that sweet unction of the Holy Spirit with which he so permeated you and made you grace-filled, that everyone who through you seeks grace finds it. Call to mind now that divine operation with which the whole Most Blessed Trinity wrought in you, when human flesh taken from your substance was so united to the Divine Nature that God was made man and man became God, and your whole soul was suffused with a sweetness and a gladness of which no human heart can conceive. And therefore every creature with rapturous admiration acknowledges and confesses that you are blessed and incomparably exalted above all creatures in heaven and on earth, and blessed the Fruit of your womb, Jesus, who quickens, sanctifies, and blesses all things forever and ever. Amen.

O Blessed Virgin Mary, you are the Mother of love, of sorrow, and of mercy. By your maternal intercession and assistance, may I always have the strength and help I need to fulfill my duties and obligations, without relaxing in the practice of the perfect love and worship that is due to God. And by your loving desire for the salvation of souls, flood my soul with your grace so that I may taste the sweetness of the Lord. I call upon you and come to you so that you may lead me to the fountain of the Divinity. Amen.

I approach you to intercede for me before the Throne of Mercy. Infuse me with your graces so that I may respond lovingly to you, receive your protection and help, and obtain the hidden manna, which will give me spiritual nourishment and life. Help me respond to your promptings so that I may follow your Son faithfully, and, by his light, contemplate more perfectly the mysteries of his Incarnation and Redemption. Help me attain that beauty of soul, which the highest King seeks in me. By your intercession and advocacy before the Throne of Mercy of your Son, who is King of kings and Lord of lords, may he, in his most powerful mercy, forgive me my sins, grant me the necessities and provisions of life, bestow graces, virtues, and spiritual blessings on me, and bring me to eternal life with him. Who lives and reigns with the Father and the Holy Spirit, one God, forever and ever. Amen.

WEEK 4: THE FOURTH SORROW OF THE BLESSED VIRGIN MARY - THE MEETING OF JESUS AND MARY WHEN HE WAS CARRYING HIS CROSS TO CALVARY

A large crowd of people followed Jesus, including many women who mourned and lamented him. (Lk. 23:27).

Day 22:   Jesus is Condemned to Death

1. Pilate Condemns Jesus to Death

When Jesus was brought before Pilate, although he found no fault with Jesus, nonetheless, he had Jesus scourged. After the scourging, the soldiers wove a crown out of thorns and placed it on his head, and clothed him in a purple cloak. They then mocked him, saying, "Hail, King of the Jews!" And they struck him repeatedly. Then Pilate took Jesus out to the people. Jesus was wearing the crown of thorns and the purple cloak. Then Pilate said to the people, "Behold, the man! I have brought him out to you so that you may know that I find no guilt in him." When the chief priests and the guards saw him they cried out, "Crucify him, crucify him!" Pilate said to them, "Take him yourselves and crucify him. I find no guilt in him." They answered, "We have a law, and according to that law he ought to die, because he made himself the Son of God."

When Pilate heard this statement, he became even more afraid, and went back into the praetorium and said to Jesus, "Where are you from?" Jesus did not answer him. So Pilate said to him, "Do you not speak to me? Do you not know that I have power to release you and I have power to crucify you?" Jesus answered him, saying, "You would have no power over me if it had not been given to you from above. For this reason the one who handed me over to you has the greater sin." Consequently, Pilate tried to release him; but they cried out, "If you release him, you are not a Friend of Caesar. Everyone who makes himself a king sets himself against Caesar." When Pilate heard these words he brought Jesus out and sat down on the judgment seat called The Stone Pavement, and in Hebrew, Gabbatha.

It was preparation day for Passover, and it was about noon. And he said to the people, "Behold, your king!" They cried out, "Take him away, take him away! Crucify him!" Pilate said to them, "Shall I crucify your king?" The chief priests answered, "We have no king but Caesar." Then he handed him over to them to be crucified.[3] Although Pilate found no fault with Jesus, nonetheless, he passed a death sentence on Jesus, the Author of life. When Mary, his Mother, heard the sentence of death by crucifixion pronounced on Jesus by Pilate, she, as any mother would, was

---

[3] Jn. 19: 1-16a.

overwhelmed by a grief beyond all human conception. Nonetheless, since she understood the redemptive purpose of his death for the human race and the benefits it would bring to souls, she was consoled.

2. Act of Reparation to the Mother of Sorrows

O Blessed Virgin Mary and Mother of Sorrows, I firmly believe with all my heart that you are the Immaculate Conception, the Mother of God, and the Queen of angels and of mortals, and that Jesus Christ, your beloved Son and our God, assumed you, body and soul, into heaven. I bless, praise, and magnify the Omnipotent God because he wrought many sacred miracles for you and, by them, you confer great helps and graces to those who invoke your aid. I hereby make reparation for those who neither believe nor acknowledge you as their Mother and Queen. I also make reparation for those who do not accept Jesus Christ as our God and Savior so that they may all come to the knowledge of the truth for the salvation of their soul and for the glory of the most holy name of God forever and ever. Amen.

O most loving Mother, I pledge my devotion to you. Watch over me and hasten to my assistance, relief, and protection in my daily life. Favor me with an abundance of your consolations and encouragements. And by your continual prayers for me, may God preserve me in the path of purity of heart and holiness. I thank you in the name of the Most High. I confess that Jesus Christ is God and Redeemer, who, for my salvation and that of the whole world, died upon the cross. I adore and call upon him, and ask him for the pardon of my sins.

O most holy Mary, Mother of my Lord and Redeemer Jesus Christ, extend your favors, graces, and strength to me and to other sinners. Pray for us, sweetest and kindest Mother, and for the other faithful of Christ so that we may always abide by the will of the Most High and so that, by our lives, we may always give glory to his most holy name. Assist us in all our difficulties and labors. O most clement Mother, bless me in the name of him who chose you among all creatures to be his Mother.

I hereby constitute you as my Advocate in the hour of my death so that I may receive your special protection against the evil one and against all his hellish hosts and attacks. So invincibly powerful are you to the dragon and all his hellish hosts that, as soon as they hear your command or feel your presence, they flee and dart in all directions back to their hellish abyss. Then safe and secure under your protection, lead my soul to the Throne of God's mercy and present me before him. And by your powerful intercession, I will be received by the Most Blessed Trinity and by all his angels and saints, and join with you and with them in praising the Father, and the Son, and the Holy Spirit, one God, forever and ever. Amen.

Day 23:   Jesus Receives His Cross

1. Jesus Carries His Cross

After Pontius Pilate had passed a death sentence on Jesus, the executioners placed the heavy cross, on which he was to be crucified, upon his Shoulders. In order that he might be able to carry it, they loosened the rope with which they had tied his hands, but not the ones they tied around his waist, since they wished to drag him to and for by the loose ends of the ropes that were bound around his waist. The cross was fifteen feet long, and made of thick and heavy timbers.

Jesus, on receiving the cross, prayed that the cross should be an altar upon which he would offer to the Everlasting Father the sacrifice of his everlasting reconciliation with the human race and that his sacrifice may be accepted by the Eternal Father. When the cross came in contact with the body of Jesus, his Mother, Mary, who saw all that was happening, venerated and adored it. The same was also done by all the angels who were invisible to everyone except Mary.

2. Act of Consolation and Compassion to Our Lady of Sorrows

O Blessed Virgin Mary, I adore and magnify your most holy Son for the love with which he delivered himself up for the salvation of the human race and for offering himself up to the Eternal Father to deliver us from the power of evil. I humbly beseech you to pray for me before your Son so that I may obtain pardon for my sins, true conversion of heart, deliverance from the evils of sin, and the fruits of his redemption. I also pray for the salvation of souls. By your intercession, may more and more people, with humble reverence, penetrate the mysteries of his redemption. Amen.

O Blessed Virgin Mother, I console you for the afflictions and torments you endured during the passion of your Son and by his death. Through your graces and guidance, may the Sun of Justice bring healing to our heart. O Mother and Queen of virtues! O true Mother of the immortal King of ages! O Mother of Sorrows, the hardness of our hearts makes us unworthy of adequately compensating you and your Divine Son for all your pains and those of his; but through your clemency make us worthy partakers of this favor. Purify us and free us from our spiritual lukewarmness whenever it arises, and obtain for us spiritual strength. Amen.

O Sacred Virgin and Mother, as a mother, you also felt in your Immaculate Heart all the pains

115

and injuries that were inflicted upon the divine Person of your Son. O what sorrow filled your heart upon seeing him denied pity and compassion and to behold him in so much bitter pains and sufferings. The image of your divine Son, wounded, disrespected, and bound remained so firmly fixed and imprinted in your soul that for the remainder of your life on earth it was never effaced, and remained in your mind as distinctly as if you were continually beholding him with your own eyes. O my Mother and Queen, behold your servant, who is dust and ashes; accept my sorrowful prayer so that it may bring relief and consolation to you and your Son, Jesus Christ our Lord, forever and ever. Amen.

Say 3 Hail Marys.

Let us pray. O Most Loving Lord Jesus Christ, by your pierced Heart and the sorrows of your Mother, pierce my heart with the arrow of your love so that nothing sinful may remain therein and so that it may be entirely filled with the strength of your Divinity. Amen.

Day 24: The Way of the Cross

1. Jesus Proceeds to Calvary with His Cross

So they took Jesus, and carrying the cross himself he went out to what is called the Place of the

Skull, in Hebrew, Golgotha.[4] Having placed the cross on his right Shoulder, Jesus proceeded on the way to Calvary. The executioners, lacking compassion and kindness, pulled our Savior Jesus along with the ropes bound around his waist with incredible cruelty. Some of them in front of him jerked him forward by the ropes that were tied around his waist in order to accelerate his passage, while those who walked behind him pulled the ends of ropes from behind in order to retard his movement. This forward and backward jerking coupled with the weight of the cross caused Jesus to sway to and fro and often to fall to the hard ground made of rough stones. By his hard fall to the ground he received on the two knees grave wounds, which widened at each repeated fall.

The heavy cross also inflicted a grievous wound on his right Shoulder on which he carried the cross. The jerking forth and back of Jesus caused by his executioners made the cross sometimes to knock against his sacred Head and, at other times, made his sacred Head to knock against the cross; as such, the spikes on the crown of thorns on his sacred Head penetrated deeper into his sacred Head. In addition to these physical torments, the soldiers also insulted him, spat on his face, and threw dirt at his face.

When they made him fall to the ground, they hardly allowed him to catch his breath before yell-

---

[4] Jn. 19: 16b-17.

ing at him to get up and continue with the walk. Having been in so few hours overwhelmed with storms of physical and psychological abuses, he was so weakened that, to all appearances, the executioners thought he was going to yield up life under his intense pains and sufferings.

2. Intercessory Prayer to the Mother of Sorrows for Single Parents

O my Sorrowful and Immaculate Mother, I present you the Sacred Heart of Jesus, your Son, which abounds in all beatitude, and I offer it to you for all single parents, especially those who are devoted to you and your Son, those who are known to me, and those who have asked me to pray for them. You know their needs and necessities; intercede for them, and grant them the help and consolation they need. Assist them with the tenderness of a mother so that they meet up with all their duties and obligations.

O Blessed Virgin Mary, compassionate Mother of sorrows! You are powerful and efficacious in obtaining results from your Son; intercede for us so that we too may obtain your assistance and speedy pardon from your Son and so that we may be strengthened in faith and grace and be protected from the evil one. You are the Mother of our Savior, and our Intercessor and Advocate before his Throne. By his death on the cross and by his precious Blood, he vanquished the power of sin and triumphed over the pride and ambitions of the ancient dragon. Do not leave us, your faithful people, to the master of lies and to ravenous wolves. O most patient and sweetest Lady of purity, extend your gentle love to us and protect us from the fury, snares, and wiles of the enemy. Let not the graces of the redemption Jesus Christ merited for us by his precious blood be in vain for us who invoke you. Let not the evil one glory in having, under your watch, vanquished your children who call to you for strength and protection. Mother of our Lord Jesus Christ, you have the compassion of a most loving Mother, look upon us with favor and love. Turn upon me your eyes of clemency, and crush the pride and vanity of the dragon. Defend us from all other dangers, preserve in us the gift of purity, guard and guide us, and bring us safely to eternal life to worship with you and all the angels and saints the Living God forever and ever. Amen.

Say 3 Hail Marys.

Let us pray. O Most High God and my Lord, behold your servant who acknowledges you as my Creator and as having been created out of nothing. I acknowledge also, O Highest Father, that your ineffable condescension with which you predestined, created, and sanctified the Blessed Virgin Mary, from all eternity, without any merits of hers, to be the Mother of your Only begotten. With my whole heart I praise and exalt your immense power, wisdom, and goodness in so favoring her. O look upon me, O kindest God and Father, and grant me eternal life. Through our Lord Jesus Christ who lives and reigns with you and the Holy Spirit, one God, forever and ever. Amen.

Day 25:   The Meeting of Jesus and Mary on His Way to Calvary

1.   Jesus and Mary Meets on the Way of Calvary

From the house of Pilate the sorrowful Mother followed, with the multitudes, Jesus on the Way of the Cross to Calvary. She was accompanied by the other pious women and by John. The surging crowds of people hindered her from getting very near to the Lord; she, therefore, asked the Eternal Father to be permitted to meet her Son on his way to Calvary to encourage and console him. She also prayed that the Eternal Father would permit her to stand at the foot of the cross of her blessed Son. The Eternal Father answered her prayers. She then asked her holy angels to make it possible for her to meet her Son on his way to Calvary. The holy angels obeyed her with great reverence and alacrity; they then led her through some bystreets to meet her Son. Thus, it came to pass that Jesus and Mary met face to face on his way to Calvary carrying his cross. When they met each other on the way to his crucifixion and death, Mother and Child looked at each other with reciprocal sorrows in their souls. They did not speak to each other, nor would the fierce cruelty of the executioners have permitted it. However, at this face to face meeting of the Prince of Peace and of the Queen of Peace, a surge of strength and energy revitalized Jesus for the onward journey to Calvary.

The most prudent Mary adored her divine Son and true God; she interiorly besought him that, since she could not relieve him of the weight of the cross and since she was not permitted to command her holy angels to lighten it, he should permit her to inspire the cruel soldiers to procure someone to help him with carrying the cross for him. This prayer was heard and answered by the Lord Jesus. Thus, in fulfillment of the prayerful wish of the Blessed Mother, the Pharisees and the executioners were inspired to engage some man to help Jesus carry the cross to Mount Calvary. At that very moment, Simon of Cyrene happened to be passing by. The soldiers seized him, and ordered him to carry the cross of Jesus. He refused at first, but he was soon compelled by the cruel and heartless soldiers to comply with their order. Jesus also gave Simon the look which melted the heart of Simon, and he became eager and willing to help Jesus carry his cross. While some of the Pharisees and the executioners allowed Simon of Cyrene to help Jesus carry his cross out of natural compassion for Jesus, others allowed it for fear that Jesus would die before he was crucified on the cross. And thus, it came to pass that they compelled a passerby, Simon of Cyrene, who was coming in from the country, the father of Alexander and Rufus, and made him carry the cross after Jesus. (Lk. 23:26).

2. Special Intention Prayer to the Mother of Sorrows

O Blessed Virgin Mary, I praise and salute you. Among all women, you are the most blessed, most fortunate, and most preferred in all nations and generations. May our Lord Jesus Christ be extolled with eternal praise, since from his exalted kingly throne he looked upon you and chose you to be his Mother. Let all generations bless him, for in no one has he magnified his name as he has done in you. O Queen of Sorrows, no one who approaches you is ever deprived of the powers of your mediation in order to obtain your gifts and graces and the eternal glory of the Most High. O Mother of the Incarnate Word, I beseech you to assist me who devoutly call on you for help in these and other intentions of mine. (*state your special intentions here*).

O Most Blessed Mother and most august Sanctuary of the Holy Spirit, I praise and salute you. I present you the Sacred Heart of Jesus, your Son, which abounds in all beatitude. I offer you all the Divine affections by which he predestined, created, and sanctified you from all eternity to be his Mother. I offer you the love and tenderness that he manifested to you on earth. I present you his tenderness toward you in the hour of his death and when, forgetting his own sorrows, he provided you with a faithful guardian, his Beloved Disciple and entrusted me to your maternal care, protection, and love through the same Beloved Disciple. I offer you the glory and honor to which he elevated you on the day of your Assumption into heaven, when you were exalted above all the choirs of angels and all the saints, and he proclaimed you Queen of heaven and earth. I offer you once more all these tokens of his love, as if he has presented them to you anew, so that you may obtain for me the forgiveness of all my sins, the remission of all the punishments and pains due to my sins, the perfect amendment of my life, the grace of your assistance with the tenderness of a mother at the hour of my death, and the gracious admittance of my soul into heaven to worship with you and all the angels and saints the Most Holy Trinity forever and ever. Amen.

V. Pray for us, O most sorrowful Virgin.

R. That we may be made worthy of the promises of Christ.

Let us pray. O Most Loving Lord Jesus, I thank you with humble and loving affection for all the blessings that I have received in abundance from you. The memory of your blessings is stored in me, and especially memorable to me are that you have entrusted me to the care and solicitude of your Blessed Mother, that you have redeemed me from the kingdom of darkness and transferred me to your Kingdom, which is a Kingdom of light, life, and love and of justice, peace, and joy in the Holy Spirit. I also thank you that you have called me to follow you, that you have drawn me closer to you, that you have dissembled and excused my sins and faults, and that you have added thereto many favors to me. O Lord Jesus, I thank you for all the blessings which you have wrought for me and for the whole human race. Amen.

Day 26: The Prayers of Mary Upon Meeting Jesus on the Way to Calvary

1. The Prayers of Mary in Meeting Jesus Carrying His Cross and the Statement of Jesus to the Women of Jerusalem

Beyond all human thought and estimation was the sorrow of the Blessed Virgin Mary when she witnessed with her own eyes her Son carrying the cross to Mount Calvary; for she alone could fittingly know and love him as True God and true Man. If God the Father had not strengthened her and preserved her life, it would have been impossible for her to live through this ordeal. With the bitterest of sorrows, she spoke to Jesus, with all sincerity and true intention, in her heart. Mary regretted that she was not able to relieve her Son and God, the light of her eyes and life of her soul, of the burden of the cross and carry it herself for him. She was prepared to die on the cross in his place for love of him; but that was not the will of the Most Holy Trinity. For it is the will of the Father that he should make the sacrifice of his life for the redemption of the human race. In the midst of so great injuries and such heinous offenses, he cherished mercy! He is charity without measure or bounds; yet he receives from people thankless return for all that he endures for their salvation and redemption from eternal damnation. The pitiable sight of Jesus and his disfigured face in which Mary saw him on the way to Calvary pierced her heart with new sorrow; it made such a deep impression on her soul that it never left her mind for the rest of her life.

And there followed him a great multitude of the people, including women who mourned and lamented for him. But turning to them Jesus said, "Daughters of Jerusalem, do not weep for me, but weep for yourselves and for your children. For behold, the days are coming when they will say, 'Blessed are the barren, the wombs that never bore, and the breasts that never nursed!' Then they will begin to say to the mountains, 'Fall on us,' and to the hills, 'Cover us.' For if they do these things when the wood is green, what will happen when it is dry?"(Lk. 23:27-31).

By these words the Lord acknowledged, appreciated, and approved of the tears that the women shed for him on account of his Passion. Jesus rewarded the women who showed compassion for him by their tears with divine enlightenment regarding the redemptive purpose of his forthcoming death and by granting them and their children the grace of repentance and everlasting life. By the words of Jesus to them, the women also understood that Jesus was telling them to weep not for him, but for their sins and for the sins of their children, because he was suffering not for himself who is innocent, but for their sins and for the sins of the human race. For the days shall come, namely the days of judgment and chastisement when those who have endured persecutions for his sake, who have repented of their sins for love of him, and who have acknowledged and appreciated the price of his blood and redemption shall be considered fortunate.

On the contrary, during the days of judgment and chastisement, unrepentant sinners shall call upon the mountains and the hills to shield them from his wrath. For if they are doing these horrible things to him when the wood is green, that is, when there is still time to repent, what will happen to them when the wood is dry, that is, when the end has come and it is too late to repent.

The Virgin Mother walked very closely behind Jesus, as she had desired and asked from the Eternal Father so as to enjoy his presence and to share more fully in all his torments and sorrows. She saw and heard the insults, blows, and reproaches they dealt him. She conformed herself in all things to the will of God. She witnessed with her own eyes all of the sufferings of her Son, and she partook of them in her soul. She never allowed any sentiment of anger to arise interiorly or exteriorly, which could have been interpreted as regret for the sacrifice she had made in offering up her Son to die on the cross for the salvation of the human race. Her charity and love of people, her merits and virtues, and her grace and holiness were so great and firm that she conquered all anger and the other disordered passions of human nature.

2. Act of Commemoration of the Seven Swords of Sorrow of the Blessed Virgin Mary

1. O Sacred Virgin Mary, I commiserate with you for the sword of sorrow that pierced your soul when Simeon said to you that a sword of sorrow shall pierce your soul. By the merits of your sufferings and sorrows, I beseech you, O Mary my Advocate, to turn on me those pitying eyes of yours and protect me with your maternal presence from all the snares of the enemy. Amen.

Say 1 Hail Mary.

2. O Holy Virgin Mary, I commiserate with you for the sword of sorrow that pierced your soul

when at the command of the angel, you fled with Joseph, your most holy spouse, and with your Beloved Son, your one and only Child, Jesus, to Egypt to escape the wrath of the murderous Herod. By the merits of your sufferings and sorrows, I beseech you, O Mary my Advocate, to turn on me those pitying eyes of yours and save my soul and obtain for me the gift of eternal life. Amen.

Say 1 Hail Mary.

3. O Loving Virgin Mary, I commiserate with you for the sword of sorrow that pierced your soul when your only Beloved Child was lost for three days until at last you found him in the temple. By the merits of your sufferings and sorrows, I beseech you, O Mary my Advocate, to turn on me those pitying eyes of yours and grant me strength against your enemies. Amen.

Say 1 Hail Mary.

4. O Admirable Virgin Mary, I commiserate with you for the sword of sorrow that pierced your soul when you saw the most pitiable countenance and disfigurement of your Beloved Christ on his way with his cross to Calvary. By the merits of your sufferings and sorrows, I beseech you, O Mary my Advocate, to turn on me those pitying eyes of yours and free me from my sins and preserve me in a state of grace. Amen.

Say 1 Hail Mary.

5. O Compassionate Virgin Mary, I commiserate with you for the sword of sorrow that pierced your soul when you beheld your Beloved Son raised high upon the cross, fastened thereto with three crude nails, and, after three long agonizing hours on the cross, he gave up the ghost. By the merits of your sufferings and sorrows, I beseech you, O Mary my Advocate, to turn on me those pitying eyes of yours and preserve, prosper, and protect all the faculties of my soul. Amen.
Say 1 Hail Mary.

6. O Blessed Virgin Mary, I commiserate with you for the sword of sorrow that pierced your soul when the Sacred Heart of your Beloved Son was pierced with a lance, and when he was taken down from the cross and placed on your maternal arms, and when you held his sacred Body close to your Immaculate Heart and bedewed it with sorrowful tears. By the merits of your sufferings and sorrows, I beseech you, O Mary my Advocate, to turn on me those pitying eyes of yours and receive my soul, as it leaves my body, into your maternal arms as you received the Body of your Son. Amen.
Say 1 Hail Mary.

7. O Immaculate Virgin Mary, I commiserate with you for the sword of sorrow that pierced your soul when your Beloved Son was buried in the Sepulcher. By the merits of your sufferings and sorrows, I beseech you, O Mary my Advocate, to

turn on me those pitying eyes of yours and pour
forth into my soul the sweetness of your maternal
love, merits, and graces and lead it up to the joys
of heaven. Amen.
Say 1 Hail Mary.

V. Sorrowful and Immaculate Heart of Mary.
R. Pray for us who have recourse to you.

Let us pray. O Eternal Father, I offer you, by
the power of the Holy Spirit, all my hurts, sufferings, and pains, and I commend them to you with
that same intention with which you brought them
down to me from the Heart of Jesus; I beseech you
to record them for me on high together with my
deepest thankfulness. Grant me a greater love for
the Sacred Heart of Jesus and the Immaculate
Heart of Mary. Amen.

Day 27: The Faithful Few Who Accompa-nied Jesus to Calvary

1. The Origin of the Way of the Cross

When Jesus was brought before Pilate, the
Mother of Jesus, John, and Magdalen stood at a
corner in the Praetorium. They were overwhelmed
with the bitterest sorrow regarding all that was
being said and done to Jesus. For example, the
chief priests and Pharisees accused him of stirring
up the people by his preaching throughout all Ju-

dea, beginning from Galilee. On hearing this, Pilate inquired whether Jesus was a Galilean. The Roman Empire at that time had divided Palestine into two principal provinces, namely: Judea and Galilee. Pilate governed Judea and Herod Galilee. Upon learning that he was under Herod's jurisdiction, he sent him to Herod who was at that time in Jerusalem, celebrating the Passover. He was the son of the first Herod who, in an attempt to procure the death of Jesus soon after his birth, had murdered innocent children. (Mt 2:16). He was also the same Herod who married Herodias, the wife of his own brother. He was also the same Herod who had John the Baptist arrested, bound, and put in prison because John the Baptist had denounced the marriage. And he was also the same Herod who had John the Baptist beheaded.[5]

Herod was very glad to see Jesus, for he had been wanting for a long time to see him. He had heard about him and had been hoping to see him perform some miracle. He questioned him at length, but Jesus gave him no answer. The chief priests and scribes, meanwhile, stood by accusing him harshly. Even Herod and his soldiers treated him with contempt and mocked him. Then, clothing him in a resplendent garment, he sent him back to Pilate.[6]

---

[5] Mk. 6: 17-29; Mt. 14:1-11; Lk. 3:18-20.
[6] Lk. 23:4-11.

When Jesus, in chains, was taken to Herod, Mary, Magdalen, and John set forth from the Praetorium and followed Jesus and the crowds to the palace of Herod. Each time they got to a spot where Jesus had fallen or where he had suffered grievously, they would weep silently at the thought of all he had undergone and revere the spot. The Blessed Virgin would kneel down and kiss the ground where her Son had fallen. Who can describe the sharp sword of grief that pierced her tender soul? She suffered with Jesus, sharing with him not only the sufferings of his bitter Passion, but also that ardent intention of the redemption of fallen humanity by his ignominious death on the cross.

The grief of Magdalen was so intense as to make her almost beside herself. The repentance she felt for her faults was immense, and not less intense was her gratitude to Christ for pardoning her sins. She beheld him betrayed, suffering, and about to die for the expiation of her offenses which he had taken upon himself.

The heart of John was filled with love, and he suffered intensely, but he uttered not a word. He supported the Mother of his beloved Master, and emulated her in venerating the ground on which Jesus had fallen or where Jesus had sanctified by his blood. This was the first Stations of the Cross, and it was introduced by the Blessed Mother, a devotion which has been continued since then by the faithful of the Church.

2. Act of Commemoration of the Joys of the Blessed Virgin Mary

1. I rejoice with you, O Blessed Virgin Mary, for that joy of yours in Heaven when, at the moment of your death, your beloved Son, Jesus, received your soul into his arms and the whole company of the heavenly saints and angels rejoiced with you on your Transition into Heaven.
Say 1 Hail Mary.

2. I rejoice with you, O Blessed Virgin Mary, for that joy of yours in Heaven when, you were assumed body and soul, by your beloved Son, Jesus, into Heaven and the whole company of the heavenly saints and angels rejoiced with you on your Assumption into Heaven.
Say 1 Hail Mary.

3. I rejoice with you, O Blessed Virgin Mary, for that joy of yours in Heaven when your beloved Son, Jesus, crowned you Queen of Heaven and Earth and the whole company of the heavenly saints and angels rejoiced with you on your Coronation in Heaven.
Say 1 Hail Mary.

4. I rejoice with you, O Blessed Virgin Mary, for that joy of yours in Heaven when you were seated at the right hand of your beloved Son, Jesus, who is seated at the right hand of the Eternal Father and the whole company of the heavenly saints and angels rejoiced with you on your Exaltation in Heaven.

Say 1 Hail Mary.

5. I rejoice with you, O Blessed Virgin Mary, for that joy of yours in Heaven when, through your intercession, a soul is released from purgatory and brought into eternal glory and the whole company of the heavenly saints and angels rejoice with you on your Intercession in Heaven.

Say 1 Hail Mary.

6. I rejoice with you, O Blessed Virgin Mary, for that joy of yours in Heaven when we call upon you in our necessities and you are liberal and generous in answering our prayers and the whole company of the heavenly saints and angels rejoice with you on your Advocacy in Heaven.

Say 1 Hail Mary.

7. I rejoice with you, O Blessed Virgin Mary, for that joy of yours in Heaven when you shall receive my soul into your most holy and protective arm and the whole company of the heavenly

saints and angels shall rejoice with you on your Joy in Heaven.

Say 1 Hail Mary.

V. Sorrowful and Immaculate Heart of Mary.
R. Pray for us who have recourse to you.

Let us pray. O Lord Jesus Christ, Immaculate Lamb of God, you died a most painful and agonizing death on the cross for the redemption of the human race. By the merits of your precious Blood and the intercession of your Blessed Mother, who stood by you in life and in death, may I amend my life and never again crucify you, my loving Redeemer, by my sins; and persevering until death in your grace, may I obtain eternal life. Amen.

Day 28: Meditations

1. The True Disciples of Christ

1. To be a true disciple of Jesus, we must deny ourselves, take up our cross, and follow him. (Mt. 16:24). There are many people who wish to follow Christ, but they are few who truly dispose themselves to imitate him; for as soon as the Lord imposes a cross on them, they cast it aside. There are many people who seek the indulgence of their passions and pleasures. They shy away from sacrifices and self-denial; they neither practice virtue nor kindness. Even when they fall into sin, they

135

make no effort to rise and continue in the path of Christian perfection. They reluctantly correct and amend their lives. They despair or find themselves unable morally to rise. The one who falls into a state of sin, but who wishes to rise to a state of grace will, with renewed efforts and ardent hope and with the help of God, overcome many difficulties, receive strength from on high, and grow in the grace of the holy fear of the Lord.

2. The grace of holy fear of the Lord arouses and stimulates the will to obey the divine commandments, to be alert in the avoidance of sin and the pursuit of eternal life, and to persevere in the friendship of God. It also helps one to receive the holy Eucharist and the other sacraments with reverence and appreciation. The sacraments are spiritual medicines for the soul, and they provide salutary effects and graces to the spiritual life of a person. And also with holy fear, one gives humble thanks to God and esteem his favors. Many people take for granted the many blessings God has bestowed upon them. God's blessings are not by virtue of our merit, and the possession of them is not a right; rather, God grants them to us because of his liberality and kindness toward his children.

3. The calmness, steadfastness, and firmness of the Blessed Virgin Mary remained unshaken in the midst of her inexpressible anguish and amidst the sorrows, sighs, and afflictions of the Passion of her divine Son. During her whole life she united

her interior dispositions and exterior occupations to the Lord. She also remained faithful to her prayers and to God. The soul that is troubled by anxiety for the things of this world or is negligent in the observance of the divine laws of God limits the abundant ways the Lord would have blessed the soul of the person. Therefore, do not permit yourself, because of your duties or other exterior occupations, to abandon your prayers and the worship due from you to God. Praise him for all that he has done for the Blessed Virgin Mary, for all that he has done for you, and for all that he has done for other souls. He manifests his goodness and infinite love to us in our daily life. Our Lord is propitious, liberal, merciful, and loving toward his children. He is the Most High and our Creator. He is our Redeemer and Best Friend forever.

2. Act of Praise to the Blessed Virgin Mary

1. Hail, O purest and holiest Mother of Jesus and our Mother, for you were chosen from all eternity to be Mother of God. I greet you, O Immaculate Conception, for you were conceived without stain of original sin. I salute you, O Virgin Mary of Nazareth, for by your *fiat* you gladly and willingly conformed to the will of God to be the Mother of the Incarnate Word. I congratulate you, O Immaculate Mary, for throughout your whole life you never committed one single sin. By your

merits and privileges, O beloved Daughter of the Eternal Father, virgin Mother of the Incarnate Word, and sacred and pure Spouse of the Holy Spirit, hear my supplications and obtain pardon for my sins.

2. O Blessed Mother of Sorrows, I call upon you to influence and assist me put an end to my sins. Your Son, our Lord Jesus Christ, is the Lord, Life, and Light of my soul! Forbid that I should be hard of heart or hostile to him or be contemptuous of him; let me be wholly obedient to his influence and inspirations. Forbid that I should ever be forgetful of his blessings or be ungrateful to him; let me be appreciative of him and be grateful to him for his countless blessings in my life. Free me and protect me from all the errors and dangers to my eternal salvation. Let your heart bear with me who has been so favored by your Son's bounty. I have often been coarse and rebellious, and cruel and ungrateful to him.

3. O Blessed Virgin Mary, Immaculate Mother of God, I praise you for the martyrdom of love and grief you endured when you beheld the sufferings and sorrows of Jesus! You co-operated in my redemption by your innumerable afflictions and by offering to the Eternal Father his only-begotten Son as a holocaust and victim of propitiation for my sins. I thank you for the unspeakable love which led you to deprive yourself of the Fruit of your womb, Jesus, true God and true Man, to save

me, a sinner. Oh! make use of the unfailing power of your intercession before the Father, the Son, and the Holy Spirit so that I may steadfastly amend my life and never again crucify my loving Redeemer by my sins and so that, persevering till death in his grace, I may obtain eternal life through the merits of his Passion and Death. Amen.

4. O Mother of God, help me pay your beloved Son and our Lord the reverence and love which he owes for his endearments. I give praise, honor, and worship to your Son and our Lord Jesus Christ, Light of light, Son of the Eternal Father, and co-substantial, co-equal, and co-eternal with the Father. I acknowledge that he is as everlasting, immense, and infinite as God, equal to him in essence and attributes, one with God, that he is holy, innocent, and without defect of any kind, the Principle that gives existence to all things, and the End that consists of my true and eternal joy, peace, love, and happiness.

5. I magnify and praise the Omnipotent God with fervent affection for the favors and riches which, beyond all human conception, his divine right hand has showered upon you. You are so fortunate and so powerful with the Almighty. O Mother of Sorrows, make me a partaker in the gifts which the Lord has placed in your hands for distribution among the faithful, raise me up from the miserable spiritual state in which I have found

myself, and enrich me with your graces to know and do what is most perfect, pleasing, and obedient to God. He chose to exalt you. I will praise the omnipotence of the Father, the wisdom of the Son, and the goodness of the Holy Spirit, one God, forever and ever. Amen.

WEEK 5: THE FIFTH SORROW OF THE BLESSED VIRGIN MARY - THE CRUCIFIXION AND DEATH OF JESUS

There they crucified him. Standing near the cross of Jesus was his mother. When Jesus saw his mother, and the disciple whom he loved standing there, he said to his mother, "Woman, behold your son." Then he said to the disciple, "Behold, your mother." (Jn. 19:18, 25-27).

Day 29: The Crucifixion of Jesus

1. Jesus is Crucified

Jesus, the Son of the Eternal Father, true God and true Man, with much effort and difficulty, reached the mountain of sacrifice, which is the same mountain to which his prototype and figure, Isaac, was brought by the patriarch Abraham for sacrifice. (Gen. 22:9). Jesus arrived at the summit of Mount Calvary weakened, exhausted, and disfigured; he was in intense pains. His sorrowful and afflicted Mother, in the bitterness of her soul, also arrived at the summit of the Mount and remained very close to her Son. She too was in deep pains not only because, as a Mother, she felt pain in her Immaculate Heart in seeing her Son in so much pain, but also because she was interiorly sharing in his pains and sufferings. Whatever blows, whips, thorns, cruelty, and pains he felt in his Sacred Body, she felt in her Immaculate Heart.

Accompanying Mary was John; for he alone of all the Apostles, through her intercession and the favor of the Eternal Father, had the privilege and blessing of remaining so constantly near to the Savior and to his cross to console the Blessed Mother. Many women who had followed Jesus from Galilee and who had given him support were also there, watching from a distance. Among them were Mary Magdalene, Mary the mother of James and Joseph, and the mother of the sons of Zebedee. (Mt. 27:55-56).

When Mary, the Mother of Jesus, perceived that the executioners were about to strip Jesus of his clothes, she approached Jesus and took hold of one of his hands, and adored and kissed it with reverence and tears. The executioners allowed her to do this because they thought that the sight of his Mother would cause him more sorrow; for they wished to spare him no sorrow. However, the Lord during his Passion had no greater source of consolation and interior joy than to see his Blessed Mother.

She then turned in spirit to the Eternal Father and prayed to him in her heart as follows: My Lord and Eternal God, you are the Father of your only-begotten Son. By eternal generation he is engendered God of the true God, namely yourself, and as man he was born of my womb; he received from me his human nature, in which he now suffers. I have nursed and sustained him at my own breast; and as the best of sons that ever can be born of any creature, I love him with maternal love. As his Mother, I have a natural right in the person of his most holy humanity and your Providence will never infringe upon the freewill and rights of any person. This right of a Mother then, I now yield to you and once more place in your hands your and my Son as a sacrifice for the redemption of the human race. Accept, my Lord, this pleasing offering, since this is more than I can ever offer by submitting my own self as a victim to suffering. This sacrifice is greater, not only because my Son is true God and of your own substance, but because this sacrifice costs me a much greater sorrow and pain. For if the lots were changed and I should be permitted to die in order to preserve his most holy life, I would consider it a great relief and the fulfillment of my dearest wishes. The Eternal Father received this prayer of Mary with ineffable complacency.

The executioners then despoiled Jesus of his outer garment and of his seamless tunic. As the tunic was without opening in the front, they pulled it over the head of Jesus without taking off the crown of thorns. On account of the rudeness with which they took off the tunic, they inhumanly tore off the crown with the tunic. They thus opened anew all the wounds of his head. And on

account of the violence with which the executioners wrenched off and despoiled him of his tunic
and, with it, the crown on his head, some of the
sharp thorns of the crown remained stuck in some
of the wounds on his head. With heartless cruelty,
they again forced down the crown of thorns upon
his head, opening up not only old wounds, but
also new wounds. Thus, they fulfilled the prophecy of David, namely that they added new pains to
his wounds (Ps. 69:27). In addition, there was the
sharp and cold wind on Mount Calvary that was
blasting ferociously against his body, which increased his sufferings.

The executioners had intended to crucify him
stark naked in the presence of his Most Blessed
Mother, of her pious companions, and of the multitudes gathered around Calvary. However, by his
divine power, Jesus reserved for himself the inner
garment, which his Mother had also sown for him.
For neither at the scourging nor at the crucifixion
could the executioners remove it; and he was laid
in the sepulcher still covered with this cloth. He
would gladly have died entirely despoiled and be-
reft of even this covering, if it had not been for the
desires and the prayers of his Blessed Mother, to
which Christ yielded. Furthermore, Christ also
used his divine power to prevent the executioners
from removing his inner garments in order to preserve and protect the holiness, chastity, and purity
of his most blessed Mother.

The executioners then commanded Christ the Lord to stretch himself upon the cross in order to be nailed to it. The King of kings, the Author of life, obeyed. He then placed himself with outstretched arms upon the blessed cross. One of the executioners then hammered a large nail through the palm of the right hand of Jesus into cross. If the ferocious, cruel, and heartless executioners had room in their hearts for the least compassion and kindness, they would not have decided to inflict further torments on him. They then took hold of his left hand and, with the chain that they had used in bounding him in the garden, they looped one end of the chain through a ring around his left hand, and, with utmost cruelty, stretched his left hand with the chain as far as it could go and fastened it with another nail to the cross. Thereupon they seized his feet, and placing them one above the other; they then tied the same chain around both of his legs and, with barbarous ferocity, nailed them to the cross.

After they had nailed Jesus to the cross, the executioners judged it necessary to bend the points of the nails which projected through the back of the cross so that the nails would not become loosened and be pulled out of the cross by the weight of the body of Jesus when he would be hanging on the cross. For this reason they raised up the top of the cross in order to turn it upside down so that Jesus would hit the ground with face downward and with the weight of the cross upon him. This new cruelty appalled all the bystanders and a shout of pity arose in the crowd. But the sorrowful and compassionate Mother intervened by her prayers, and asked the Eternal Father not to permit this cruel outrage to happen in the way the executioners had intended. She commanded her guardian angels to come to the assistance of Jesus. When, therefore, the executioners raised up the cross to let it fall so that the face of Jesus would hit the ground, the holy angels supported him and the cross above the stony ground so that his divine countenance did not come in contact with the sharp rocks and edges on the ground. The executioners, totally ignorant of this miracle, bent over the points of the nails. His body was so near to the ground and the cross was so firmly held by the angels that the people thought it rested upon the hard rock.

They then lifted up the upper end of the cross with Jesus nailed to it, dragged it to the hole in the ground which they had prepared, and positioned the foot of the cross into the hole. It was already the sixth hour, which corresponds to noontime. Thus, Jesus, true God and true Man, was made to hang on the cross in full view of the innumerable multitudes of different nations and countries, of his pious followers, and of his Blessed Mother. He shed much blood from the nail wounds, which had widened when the end of the cross was let into the hole in the ground. They also crucified the two thieves, one to the right of Jesus and the other to his left. The passers-by hurled insults at him. They shook their heads in scorn and mockery. They said to him, saying: Ah you, who said you would destroy the temple and rebuild it in three days, save yourself! If you are the Son of God, come down from the cross. The chief priests, the Pharisees, and the elders, forgetting about the two thieves, turned all the venom of their fury against Jesus and mocked him saying: He saved others, but he cannot save himself; if this be the Son of God let him come down from the cross, and we will believe in him. He trusts in God; let God deliver him now; for he said, I am God's Son. They thus fulfilled the scripture written about Jesus: I am scorned by men, despised by the people. All who see me mock me. They curl their lips, they shake their heads, saying: He trusted in the Lord, let him save him; let the Lord deliver him if this is his friend. (Psa. 22:6-8).

The two thieves in the beginning also mocked Jesus, saying: If you are the Son of God, save yourself and us. (Mt. 27:39-44). These blasphemies, like arrows, pierced the heart of both Jesus and Mary. These blasphemies of the two thieves, however, caused special sorrows to our Lord because these two thieves were so near to death and were losing the grace of his eternal redemption for them.

Through the intercession of the Blessed Virgin Mary, one of them, however, availed himself of the greatest opportunity that a sinner ever had in this world, and was converted from his sins. Then he rebuked the other criminal saying: Have you no fear of God? You are under the same sentence of condemnation. And indeed, we have been condemned justly, for the sentence we have received corresponds to our crimes; but this man has done nothing wrong. Then he said: Jesus, remember me when you come into your kingdom. And Jesus replied to him, saying: Amen, I say to you, this day you will be with me in Paradise. (Lk. 23:39-43).

According to a custom which permitted the executioners to take possession of the property of those whom they have executed, the executioners then proceeded to divide the garments of Jesus. The cloak or outside mantle, which his Blessed Mother had made for him and which was the one Christ had laid aside at the washing of the feet, they tore into four parts and divided among themselves. (Jn. 19:23). However, by a mysterious decree of Divine Providence, they did not divide the seamless tunic, which his Mother had also made for him; rather, they drew lots to see whose it shall be. And they gave the sacred tunic, whole and entire, to the one among them who won it. And thus they fulfilled the prophecy of David, which says: they divided my garments among them; for my clothing they cast lots. This is what the soldiers did. Standing by the cross of Jesus was his Mother.[7]

2. Act of Reparation to the Mother of Sorrows

Litany of Our Lady of Sorrows

Lord, have mercy. Lord, have mercy.
Christ, have mercy. Christ, have mercy.
Lord, have mercy. Lord, have mercy.
Christ, hear us. Christ, graciously hear us.
God the Father of heaven, have mercy on us.
God the Son, Redeemer of the world, have mercy on us.
God the Holy Spirit, have mercy on us.
Holy Mary, Mother of God, pray for us.
Holy Virgin of virgins, pray for us.
Mother of the Crucified, pray for us.
Sorrowful Mother, pray for us.
Mournful Mother, pray for us.
Sighing Mother, pray for us.
Afflicted Mother, pray for us.
Forsaken Mother, pray for us.
Desolate Mother, pray for us.
Mother most sad, pray for us.
Mother set around with anguish, pray for us.
Mother overwhelmed by grief, pray for us.
Mother transfixed by a sword, pray for us.

---

[7] Ps. 22:19; Mt. 27: 35; Jn. 19:24-25.

Mother crucified in your heart, pray for us.
Mother bereaved of your Son, pray for us.
Sighing Dove, pray for us.
Mother of Sorrows, pray for us.
Fount of tears, pray for us.
Sea of bitterness, pray for us.
Field of tribulation, pray for us.
Mass of suffering, pray for us.
Mirror of patience, pray for us.
Rock of constancy, pray for us.
Remedy in perplexity, pray for us.
Joy of the afflicted, pray for us.
Ark of the desolate, pray for us.
Refuge of the abandoned, pray for us.
Shield of the oppressed, pray for us.
Conqueror of the incredulous, pray for us.
Solace of the wretched, pray for us.
Medicine of the sick, pray for us.
Help of the faint-hearted, pray for us.
Strength of the weak, pray for us.
Protectress of those who fight, pray for us.
Haven of the shipwrecked, pray for us.
Calmer of tempests, pray for us.
Companion of the sorrowful, pray for us.
Retreat of those who groan, pray for us.
Terror of the treacherous, pray for us.
Standard-bearer of the Martyrs, pray for us.
Treasure of the Faithful, pray for us.
Light of Confessors, pray for us.
Pearl of Virgins, pray for us.

Comfort of Widows, pray for us.
Joy of all Saints, pray for us.
Queen of your Servants, pray for us.
Holy Mary, who alone are beyond compare, pray for us.
V. Pray for us, most Sorrowful Virgin.
R. That we may be made worthy of the promises of Christ.

Let us pray. O God, in whose Passion, according to the prophecy of Simeon, a sword of grief pierced through the most sweet soul of your glorious Blessed Virgin Mother Mary, grant that we, who celebrate the memory of her seven sorrows, may obtain the happy effect of your Passion, who lives and reigns world without end. Amen.

Day 30: The First and Second Last Words of Jesus

1. Father, Forgive Them for They Know Not What They Do

The first, last words of Jesus on the cross: Father, forgive them, for they know not what they do. (Lk. 23:34). By these words, Jesus not only pardoned his enemies, but he also excused their malice and blind ignorance in persecuting, blaspheming, and crucifying their God and Redeemer. Also by these words, Christ our Lord was also addressing the Eternal Father that he is the Son of

God the Father, that he is true God with the Father and the Holy Spirit, that he has permitted death in his most sacred and perfect humanity, that he has united his Divinity to human nature for the salvation of the whole human race, and that he now offers his infinitely precious life for the pardon of the sins of all those children of Adam, who should avail themselves of the redemption he has wrought for the human race. By these words, Jesus was also putting into practice his teachings on the forgiveness of others.

By this prayer, Jesus was also beseeching our heavenly Father to withhold his chastisement and not to raise the scourge of his justice over poor sinners so that they are not punished as they deserve. Psalm 130, says: If you, O Lord, should mark our guilt, Lord, who would survive? But with you is found forgiveness; for this we revere you and with the Lord there is mercy and fullness of redemption.[8]

By the first of his seven last words on the cross, Jesus was also beseeching the Eternal Father to help us ponder on the death of Jesus. By these words, Jesus also prayed for his persecutors and enemies so that they may be converted to truth for the salvation of their soul and for the honor and glory of the Most Holy Trinity.

This prayer of our Savior Jesus was perfectly understood by the Blessed Virgin Mary, and she

---

[8] Psa. 130: 3-4, 7b.

152

imitated him by forgiving the people who have condemned and crucified her Son.

2. Today, You Shall Be with me in Paradise

The second, last words of Jesus on the cross: This day you shall be with me in Paradise. (Lk. 23:43). One of the two thieves, Dismas, became aware of the mysteries of the redemption wrought for the human race by Jesus. He came to the knowledge of this divine mystery through the intercession of most holy Mary, and he was interiorly enlightened concerning the first words of Jesus on the cross. Moved by true sorrow and contrition for his sins, he turned to his companion and said: do you not fear God, seeing that you are under the same condemnation? We have been indeed condemned justly, for we receive the due reward of our crimes; but this Man has done no evil. And thereupon speaking to Jesus, he said: Lord, remember me when you shall come into your kingdom! (Lk. 23:40). And Jesus turned to him, and replied: Amen, I say to you, this day you shall be with me in Paradise. By these words, Jesus not only assured the good thief of eternal paradise, but also the rest of humanity so that if we should repent of our sins and amend our life, we shall likewise receive his mercy and the grace of eternal life.

Furthermore, by these second, last words of Jesus, the gates of paradise, which had been closed against people because of the first sin was henceforth opened so that people can enter therein and take possession of their heavenly mansions; for in his Father's house, there are many mansions. (Jn. 14:2).

By these words, Jesus was also saying that the fruits of the redemption and justification of sinners by means of his most precious Blood have commenced. The merits of the Incarnation, Passion, and Death of Jesus Christ have commenced with new force and strength such that human nature, which had fallen as a result of the first sin, has now been exalted to the highest dignity and to the favor of God, and that this restoration of the human race to the friendship and favor of God is the work of the infinite mercy of God the Father and God the Holy Spirit through the Person of God the Son. The power of Christ to call sinners and to free them from their sins and to grant them eternal life is now acting on the human race, and that people can be saved by calling upon the name of Jesus and by living good and holy life.

3. Act of Consolation and Compassion to the Mother of Sorrows

O Mary, who has a crown of twelve stars on your head, who has for a footstool under your feet the moon, and who has for your throne the wings of angels, turn your eyes of pity upon me in this valley of sorrows, and listen to the voice of one who reposes trust and confidence in you. I have sorrows which try me, pains which overwhelm me, temptations which test me, and wounds which hurt me. I have recourse to you, as to a port of safety, to a fount of complete refreshment, and to a fortress of protection. When the waves of life lash themselves with fury against me; I turn to you for calm, compassion, and consolation. When the whirlwind of life blows against me, I have recourse to you for peace, prosperity, and protection. You are consolation and refreshment for my soul, for you are the Queen of Heaven and Earth, you are my most blessed Mother and Queen.

O Mary, Mother of all creatures, enlighten my mind and touch my heart, so that the most pure love which streams from your Immaculate Heart may be poured forth on me, and produce those marvelous graces in my life for which your Son shed his most precious Blood, while you suffered with him the most cruel pangs at the foot of the cross. I beseech you also, that I may be divinely helped to ponder upon the death of your Son, Jesus Christ, in pious affection and be enlightened from above. Above all, I ask for the exultation of the ineffable and most holy name of God. Amen.

V. Sorrowful and Immaculate Heart of Mary.

R. Pray for us who have recourse to you.

Let us pray. O Jesus, heavenly Physician, I recall with devotion and love the anguish and pain you endured when lifted upon the cross, with your blessed Mother at the foot of the Cross, when all your bones were out of joint, so that no sorrow was like to your sorrow, because there were pains in you from the crown of your Head to the soles of your Feet. Nevertheless, you put away the feeling of all your own griefs, and prayed to your Father for your enemies, saying: Father, forgive them; for they know not what they do. By this your charity and your mercy, grant that the dignity and worth of your Passion may be the entire remission of all my sins. Amen.

O Lord Jesus, Mirror of the eternal splendor, remember that sadness which filled your heart when you beheld in the mirror of your Divinity the depth of your compassion for lost souls and despairing sinners. By the mercy you showed to the robber on the cross, saying: This day you shall be with me in Paradise, I beseech you, O Compassionate Jesus, show me your mercy in the hour of my death. Amen.

Day 31:   The Third Last Words of Jesus

1. Woman, Behold Your Son; Behold Your Mother

The third, last words of Jesus on the cross: Woman, behold your son. Behold your Mother (Jn. 19:26). Mary and John were standing at the foot of the cross. Jesus gazed upon his Mother, and she at him. When the eyes of both Mother and Son met, streams of tears gushed forth from her eyes. And when Jesus saw the sorrow and pain in the heart of his Mother, it caused him further pain. Then he said to her: Woman, behold your son! And then to the Beloved Disciple, he said: Behold your Mother!

Jesus addressed his Mother, "Woman," for three reasons. One, to confirm that Mary is the woman whose image and prophetic vision God had shown to all the angels in the heavens at their creation, but which Lucifer and his apostate angels had refused to venerate. Two, to confirm that Mary is the woman who is mentioned in Genesis and who is destined by God to crush the head of the serpent. (Gen. 3:15). And three, to confirm that Mary is the woman who is most blessed among all women. (Lk. 1:42).

By the words of Jesus to his Mother, Jesus was also saying that he is going to the Father and Mary cannot accompany him now; therefore, his Beloved Disciple would attend to her and care for her as his Mother, for he would be a son to her. And by his words to his Beloved Disciple, Jesus was instructing him to take Mary as his Mother. Mary had lost her most holy spouse, Joseph, and she was about to lose her only Child; therefore, his Beloved Disciple must be a son to her and she will be a Mother to him.

When Jesus said to his Beloved Disciple: Behold your Mother, he gave us over to his Mother, Mary, not only as a role model for us, but also as our powerful intercessor and advocate, after the Holy Spirit, before her beloved Son. The Apostle, on his part, received her as his own Mother from that hour onwards. He became enlightened anew and understood more profoundly and appreciated more deeply that Mary is the greatest treasure of the Three Persons in God after the humanity of Christ our Savior. In this light, he reverenced and cared for her for the rest of her life. Our Lady also accepted him as her son. John, the beloved disciple of Jesus, represents every other beloved disciple of Jesus. The Bible says that from the moment Jesus told his Beloved Disciple to take Mary as his Mother, the beloved disciple took her into his home. (Jn. 19:27). This points out to all other beloved disciples of Jesus to take the Blessed Virgin Mary, the Mother of Jesus, as their Most Blessed Mother and to make room for her both in their heart and in their home. Mary also accepted him as her son; just as she accepts as her children all those who take her as their Mother and invoke her help.

2. Intercessory Prayer for Children and Young People

O Sorrowful Mother, by your tears, by the crown of thorns, by the nails that you carry in your hand, by the swords of sorrow with which our sins transpierced your heart, turn your eyes of mercy toward children and young people. Obtain from your Most Holy Son protection for them, nourishment for their body and soul, and lively sentiments of faith, hope, and charity for them. O Sorrowful Mother, protect the holy Church, protect our country, protect our children and youth, and protect my family and I. Amen.

O Blessed Virgin Mary, your Beloved Son, Jesus, has entrusted me to you to be my Most Blessed Mother. O Queen of all created things in heaven and on earth; you are my Most Blessed Mother, the Mother of all creatures, the Mother of piety, the Intercessor of the faithful, the Advocate of sinners, the Mother of beautiful love and holy hope. You are mighty in drawing the will of the Most Blessed Trinity to mercy and clemency. You are the perfect work of the hands of God, and the plenitude of God's graces and blessings. All who call upon you from their heart shall not perish; all who obtain your intercession secure for themselves eternal life. O Holy Mary, you have been exalted high above all human and angelic creatures. O Virgin Mary, Mother of prudence, I pray you to grant me prudence. Plead for me before the throne of the Holy Spirit so that he may grant me the seven gifts of the Holy Spirit. O Loving Mother, I humbly beseech you for divine Intervention in all my affairs, for your maternal peace, blessings, protection, and wisdom, and for the grace to be a holy and faithful to God. Come to my aid; with you comes all good things and countless riches with which you bless those who invoke you and trust in you. Take upon yourself anew the care of my soul until at last I am safely in heaven to join with you and all the angels and saints in adoring the Most Blessed Trinity forever and ever. Amen.

V. Sorrowful and Immaculate Heart of Mary.

R. Pray for us who have recourse to you.

Let us pray. O Jesus, King most beloved, remember all the mournful desolation of your heart, when you, the most tender and most faithful of friends, was forsaken by all, and mocked as you hung on the cross; when you found none to comfort you but your beloved Mother, who stood by your cross to the last, and whom you commended to your disciple, saying: Woman, behold your son; and to the disciple: Behold your Mother. I beseech you, O Compassionate Jesus, by that sword of anguish which then pierced her heart, do comfort and console me in all my tribulations. Amen.

Day 32:   The Fourth Last Words of Jesus

1. My God, my God, Why have You Forsaken Me

The fourth, last words of Jesus on the cross: My God, my God, why have you forsaken me? (Mt. 27:46). Already the ninth hour of the day, or three o'clock in the afternoon, was approaching. There was already darkness on the face of the earth. Je-

160

sus then spoke the fourth word from the cross in a loud and strong voice so that all the bystanders could hear it. He said: My God, my God, why have you forsaken me? Although Jesus had uttered these words in his own native language of Aramaic, (*Eli, Eli, lema sabachthani*), which the people could understand and although he had uttered it loud, strong, and clear so that everyone could hear him, nonetheless, some of them thought he was calling on Elijah. Therefore, a number of them mocked him saying: He is calling on Elijah. Let us see whether Elijah will come and take him down. (Mk. 15:35-36).

The abandonment by the Father which Christ speaks about is that which he in his humanity. Inasmuch as Jesus is True God, it is impossible for him as God to be forsaken by God the Father since the divinity of Christ is inseparably one with the divinity of God the Father. "The Father and I are one." (Jn. 10:30). Furthermore, God the Father showed his concern for Christ by causing darkness to come over the whole land from about noon until three in the afternoon (Lk. 23:44) to give witness to the death of his Son, Jesus. Another reason why Jesus said he was forsaken by God is to let us know that although we may sometimes feel forsaken by God, nonetheless, God is always with us.

The deep science and enlightenment concerning the ever-abiding presence of God in the life of those who feel forsaken by God was perfectly known to Mary who stood at the foot of the cross and who began interiorly to beseech people to understand that God is always with them. Thus, says the Lord: Can a mother forget her infant, and be without compassion for the child of her womb? Even if she should forget, I will never forget you. (Isa. 49:15). Behold, I am with you always until the end of time. (Mt. 28:20).

2. Special Intention Prayer to Our Mother of Sorrows

1. O Blessed Virgin Mary and Mother of the Incarnate Word, your most holy name is gravely feared by the evil one and all his apostate angels. I beseech you, by the virtues in your most holy name and in the name of Jesus, to protect me from evil and from heresies, deceptions, pride, and vainglory, to obtain pardon for all my offenses, and to unite all my thoughts, words, and works indissolubly and powerfully to you. May all those graces which I have lost because of my sins and weaknesses be supplied through that boundless love you have for the Most Holy Trinity. Through the divine operations of the Holy Spirit, grant me the virtues of compassion, humility, perseverance, patience, and strength to enable me to endure my pains and sufferings; and, if it be the will of God, to grant me divine and emotional healing. I have not honored and reverenced the name of Jesus and your name as I should, and I have offended the

162

goodness of God so many times by my thoughts, words, and actions. Look upon me with your serene and loving countenance, and oblige me with God's forgiveness and yours, and grant me mighty strength and protection. Amen.

2. O Mother of mercy, the Fount of forgiveness has been given to you by your Son, so that you may obtain grace for us from him and so that the multitude of our sins and our deficiencies might be covered by your abundant charity. Beseech the Almighty God to, in his mercy, strengthen and protect me against the manipulations and machinations of the powers of darkness. Let my petition for the salvation of my soul reach your Immaculate Heart, and grant me the power of your love and compassion. You know that I have been assailed numerous times by infernal attacks. But thanks be to your faithfulness and protection, O my Blessed Mother, who are the Mother of the true God and true Man, you have strengthened and protected me in my spiritual battles, you have advanced me in virtue, and you have won victories for me. To you, I come and I invoke your divine assistance for the following special intentions of mine. (*state your intentions here*).

3. May the most sweet and divine charity of your Immaculate Heart, the abundant tenderness of your divine Motherhood, and the power and virtues in your most holy name intercede for me and obtain for me not only pardon for all my sins,

but also your assistance and favors, and your strength and protection now and at the hour of my death. Amen.

V. Pray for us, O most sorrowful Virgin.

R. That we may be made worthy of the promises of Christ.

Let us pray. O Most Loving Lord Jesus, I thank you with humble and loving affection for all the blessings that I have received in abundance from you. The memory of your blessings is stored in me, and especially memorable to me are that you have entrusted me to the care and solicitude of your Blessed Mother, that you have redeemed me from the kingdom of darkness and transferred me to your Kingdom, which is a Kingdom of light, life, and love and of justice, peace, and joy in the Holy Spirit. I also thank you that you have called me to follow you, that you have drawn me closer to you, that you have dissembled and excused my sins and faults, and that you have added thereto many favors to me. O Lord Jesus, I thank you for all the blessings which you have wrought for me and for the whole human race. Amen.

O Jesus, mighty King, by the merits of the depths of the bitter pains of your Passion when you felt forsaken by your Father, and which made you to cry out with a loud voice, saying: My God, my God, why have you forsaken me, I beseech you, to not forsake me in my last agony, but to be with me and to bring my soul to your kingdom of heavenly glory to praise you, and the Father, and the Holy Spirit, one God, forever and ever. Amen.

Day 33: The Fifth and Sixth Last Words of Jesus

1. I Thirst

The fifth, last words of Jesus on the cross: I thirst. (Jn. 19:28). The sufferings of Jesus on the cross caused his natural thirst for water. But his thirst was not actually for natural water, but for the salvation of souls. He is athirst for the salvation of the soul of everyone so that we may, by his passion and death, gain his friendship and the grace of the eternal happiness he has acquired for us. His last will and testament is that all should be saved and inherit the kingdom prepared for us since the foundation of the world. This spiritual thirst of our Savior was perfectly understood by the most blessed Mary and she began, with ardent affection and charity, to invite and interiorly call upon everyone to approach their Savior and thus quench, at least in part, his thirst for the salvation of their soul which they could not on their own quench.

But some of the people, thinking that he was asking for water, fastened to a reed a sponge soaked in gall and vinegar and raised it to his mouth, in order that he might drink of it. Thus was fulfilled the prophecy of David: In my thirst they gave me vinegar to drink. (Jn. 16:28; Ps. 68:22). Also, taking a cue from the words of Solomon, who said: Give strong drink to the sorrowful and wine to those that suffer bitterness of heart (Prov. 31:6), it was customary at that time to give to those who were about to be executed a drink of strong and aromatic wine in order to raise their vital spirits and to help them bear their torments with greater fortitude. However, this custom was perverted in the case of Jesus in order to increase his pains and sufferings (Prov. 3:6). Thus, the drink, which was intended to assist and strengthen other criminals, was mixed with gall, in the case of Jesus, so that it should have no other effect than to torment his sense of taste by its bitterness.

Mary perceived that the impious soldiers were preparing to give to the Lord a drink of wine, myrrh, and gall. Thus, the Blessed Mother, aware of their evil intentions, prayed to Jesus, in her maternal tender and compassionate heart, to not drink of it. Jesus in deference to the petition of his Mother, without rejecting entirely this new suffering, tasted of the mixture, but would not drink it entirely (Mt. 27:34).

2. It is Accomplished

The sixth, last words of Jesus on the cross: It is accomplished. (Jn. 19:29). Jesus pronounced the sixth word: It is accomplished. By these words,

Jesus is saying that his purpose of coming down from heaven to earth has been accomplished, that his mission on earth has been accomplished, that he has accomplished the will of the Father, who sent him to suffer and die for the salvation of the human race, and that he is returning to the Father.

Christ our Redeemer has obediently fulfilled the will of the Eternal Father and accomplished all the promises and prophecies made by the ancient Fathers. His humility and obedience have compensated for the pride and disobedience of Lucifer and his fellow fallen angels who refused to subject themselves and acknowledge Jesus as their God in human flesh; and the wisdom and power of God has justly humbled and vanquished them by the very Lord whom they despised and rejected. In addition, Our Lord, in obedience to the Eternal Father, has vanquished pride and the other capital sins. By prayer and the grace of God, by living faith, unwavering hope, and patient endurance, by dignified humility, and by the practice of virtues and the faithful worship of God shall we conquer pride and the other vices.

Mary not only heard these words of Jesus, but she also understood its meaning. The reason he was formed of human nature by the power of the Holy Spirit in her most sacred and virginal womb was for him to come into the world in order to suffer and die for the salvation of the human race. He has accomplished his mission on earth, he has established the Church with its sacraments and doctrines, and he obtained the forgiveness of sins for the human race. Mary also understood these last words of Jesus to mean that Jesus, having accomplished the whole purpose of his Incarnation and Death, is inviting everyone to partake of his friendship and kindness and he would secure for them eternal life.

3. Act of Commemoration of the Seven Sorrows of the Blessed Virgin Mary

1. O most holy and afflicted Virgin Mary! I console you for the sorrow that pierced your maternal heart when, on presenting your divine Son in the temple in Jerusalem, the holy Simeon foretold that a sword would pierce your heart, thereby announcing the share you would have in the sufferings of your dear Son. I beseech you, O glorious Queen of Angels, to obtain for me, through the sufferings of Jesus Christ, a sincere disdain for sin and the perfect amendment of my life under your special care and protection. Amen.

2. O most holy and blessed Virgin! I console you for the sorrow that pierced your maternal heart when you were obliged to flee into Egypt with Joseph and your Divine Infant to save him from the fury of Herod. I beseech you, O glorious Queen of Virgins, to obtain for me, through the sufferings of Jesus Christ, an ardent love of God under your special care and protection. Amen.

3. O most holy and sacred Virgin! I console you for the sorrow that pierced your maternal heart when you were separated from your Divine Son, who remained for three days absent from you after your journey to Jerusalem. I beseech you, O glorious Queen of Apostles, to obtain for me, through the sufferings of Jesus Christ, a holy life under your special care and protection. Amen.

4. O most holy and compassionate Virgin! I console you for the sorrow that pierced your maternal heart when you saw your pitiable and disfigured Son with his heavy cross on the way to Mount Calvary, and beheld him sinking under the weight of the cross of our sins. I beseech you, O glorious Queen of Martyrs, to obtain for me, through the sufferings of Jesus Christ, a faithful devotion to you under your special care and protection. Amen.

5. O most holy and sorrowful Virgin! I console you for the sorrow that pierced your maternal heart when you stood near the cross of Jesus, and witnessed all his torments and agony, and saw him at last expire for the sins of the world. I beseech you, O glorious Queen of Confessors, to obtain for me, through the sufferings of Jesus Christ, perfect health of mind and body under your special care and protection. Amen.

6. O most holy and loving Virgin! I console you for the sorrow that pierced your maternal heart when the sacred Side of your Son dear and

divine was pierced with a lance, his adorable Body was taken down from the cross, and when he was laid in your arms and you bedewed it with tears. I beseech you, O glorious Queen of Pastors, to obtain for me, through the sufferings of Jesus Christ, a pure and holy soul under your special care and protection. Amen.

7. O most holy and kind Virgin! I console you for the sorrow that pierced your maternal heart when the sacred Body of your most innocent Jesus was taken from your arms, when he was led in procession to his burial place, and when he laid in the Sepulcher. I beseech you, O glorious Queen of Heaven, to obtain for me, through the sufferings of Jesus Christ, a holy death under your special care and protection. Amen.

V. By the virtue of your pains and sufferings, O most sorrowful Virgin,

R. Incorporate me wholly into the most sacred wounds and blood of our Lord Jesus Christ!

Let us pray. O Jesus, Innocent Lamb of God and inexhaustible Fountain of pity, with the gratitude of every creature of your hands I give you thanks for the bitter thirst you suffered for the salvation of the world, when with a loud voice you exclaimed: I thirst; and when nothing was given you to drink but only vinegar and gall. I beseech you by the bitterness of that thirst to forgive me all the sins which I have ever committed against you by immoderate eating and drinking. Amen.

I praise you, O Compassionate Jesus, through your sweetest Heart, for the firm and assured hope with which your most blessed Mother, Mary the celestial Virgin, thought only of glorifying you by the purity of her intentions; in which she imitated you when, at the sixth hour of the day, you, being suspended on the tree of the cross, in all the bitterness and anguish of death, longed with your whole soul for the redemption of the human race, crying out: I thirst. For what did you thirst, O Loving Jesus, but for the salvation of the soul of every person; so that, had it been necessary for you to suffer more bitter or cruel torments, you would willingly have borne them for our redemption. Amen.

O Jesus, strong Lion of the tribe of Judah, remember now the sorrow and the suffering you endured, when all the forces of your Heart and of your Flesh failed you utterly, and bowed your Head and cried out: It is accomplished. By this your anguish and your pain, have mercy on me at the end of my life when my soul shall depart my body, and my spirit disquieted within me. And by the virtues, merits, and graces contained in your sacred words that it is completed and by which you completed the works of our salvation, may my soul, when my time on earth is complete, be cleansed and purified of its sins, be granted remission of all the pains and punishments due to my sins, and be granted everlasting joy in your heavenly kingdom forever and ever. Amen.

Day 34:   The Seventh Last Words of Jesus

1. Father into Your Hands I Commend My Spirit

The seventh, last words of Jesus on the cross: Father, into your hands I commend my spirit. (Lk. 23:46). Having come from the Father and entered mortal life through birth (Jn. 16:8), having accomplished in the flesh his mission on earth, and having established the work of our redemption, Jesus knew that it was time he returned to the Father and entered immortal life through death. Therefore, Christ our Savior, addressing the Father, said: Father, into your hands I commend my spirit. The Lord spoke these words in a loud and strong voice such that all the bystanders heard him. In pronouncing these words, Jesus raised up his eyes to heaven, as one speaking to the Eternal Father, and, with his last breath, he gave up the ghost and inclined his Head. By the divine force of these last, seventh words of Jesus, Lucifer with all his demons were hurled into the deepest caverns of hell. Through the death of Jesus on the cross, God has opened the gates of paradise to all. While we were dead in our sins, God gave us new life through Christ by forgiving us all our sins and by erasing the record of our sins with all its consequences that stood against us; he took them away, nailing them to the cross. He vanquished the principalities and the powers; he made a public spectacle of them, triumphing over them by the cross.[9]

Jesus said these last words of his, namely: "Father, into your hands I commend my spirit," to teach us that we should in life, and especially at the hour of death, commend our spirit into the hands of our heavenly Father. These words and prayers of Christ are powerful in protecting us from temptations and despair, in summoning the angels of God to our aid, and in saving our soul.

Mary, the Mother of Jesus, felt and suffered in her Immaculate Heart the pangs and agony of the death of her Son, Jesus, as though she herself had died. This last pain of hers was more intense, more excruciating, and more painful than all the others. All the pains that the martyrs and other saints have suffered and all that future martyrs and other saints will ever suffer shall never equal what the Blessed Virgin Mary suffered during the passion and death of her Son, Jesus. If God the Father had not preserved her life, she would have died at that instance.

---

[9] Col. 2:13-15.

2. Act of Commemoration of the Joys of the Blessed Virgin Mary

1. Most Holy Trinity, Father, Son, and Holy Spirit, we adore you, and with all the love of our whole hearts we give you thanks for the high gifts and privileges granted to Mary most holy in her glorious and Immaculate Conception.

2. Most Holy Trinity, Father, Son, and Holy Spirit, we adore you, and with all the love of our whole hearts we give you thanks for the high gifts and privileges granted to Mary in her glorious Nativity.

3. Most Holy Trinity, Father, Son, and Holy Spirit, we adore you, and with all the love of our whole hearts we give you thanks for the high gifts and privileges granted to Mary most holy in her glorious and most sweet name of Mary.

4. Most Holy Trinity, Father, Son, and Holy Spirit, we adore you, and with all the love of our whole hearts we give you thanks for the high gifts and privileges granted to Mary most holy in her glorious Purification in the Temple.

5. Most Holy Trinity, Father, Son, and Holy Spirit, we adore you, and with all the love of our whole hearts we give you thanks for the high gifts and privileges granted to Mary most holy in her glorious Betrothal to Joseph.

6. Most Holy Trinity, Father, Son, and Holy Spirit, we adore you, and with all the love of our whole hearts we give you thanks for the high gifts

and privileges granted to Mary most holy in her glorious Annunciation.

7. Most Holy Trinity, Father, Son, and Holy Spirit, we adore you, and with all the love of our whole hearts we give you thanks for the high gifts and privileges granted to Mary most holy in her glorious Visitation.

8. Most Holy Trinity, Father, Son, and Holy Spirit, we adore you, and with all the love of our whole hearts we give you thanks for the high gifts and privileges granted to Mary most holy in her glorious and virginal Motherhood.

9. Most Holy Trinity, Father, Son, and Holy Spirit, we adore you, and with all the love of our whole hearts we give you thanks for the high gifts and privileges granted to Mary most holy in her glorious Presentation of Jesus at the Temple.

10. Most Holy Trinity, Father, Son, and Holy Spirit, we adore you, and with all the love of our whole hearts we give you thanks for the high gifts and privileges granted to Mary most holy at the descent of the Holy Spirit upon her and the Apostles on Pentecost Day.

11. Most Holy Trinity, Father, Son, and Holy Spirit, we adore you, and with all the love of our whole hearts we give you thanks for the high gifts and privileges granted to Mary most holy in her glorious Assumption body and soul into Heaven.

12. Most Holy Trinity, Father, Son, and Holy Spirit, we adore you, and with all the love of our

whole hearts we give you thanks for the high gifts and privileges granted to Mary most holy in her glorious Coronation as Queen of Heaven and Earth.

V. Mother of love, of compassion, and of mercy.

R. Pray for us that we may be made worthy of the promises of Christ.

Let us pray. O Jesus, Splendor of the Father's glory and Figure of his substance, I recall with devotion and love that earnest commendation with which you commended your spirit to the Father, saying: Father, into your hands I commend my spirit! And when, your Sacred Body was torn and your Heart broken, and all the depth of your compassion was laid bare for our redemption, you gave up the spirit. I beseech you by that love which moved you, the Life of all that live, to submit to death, and by the sorrows and sufferings of your most Holy Mother, the Blessed Virgin Mary, that you would mortify and cast out of my soul whatever is displeasing to you and instill in me those virtues you desire of me. Amen.

My crucified Jesus, mercifully accept the prayer which I now make to you for help in the moment of my death, when at its approach all my senses shall fail me. When therefore, O sweetest Jesus, my weary and downcast eyes can no longer look up to you, be mindful of the loving gaze which now I turn on you, and have mercy on me.

When my parched lips can no longer kiss your most sacred wounds, remember then those kisses which now I imprint on your sacred Wounds, and have mercy on me. When my cold hands can no longer embrace your cross, forget not the affection with which I embrace it now, and have mercy on me. And when, at length, my swollen and lifeless tongue can no longer speak, remember that I called upon you now.

Jesus, Mary, and Joseph, I give you my heart and my soul. Jesus, Mary, and Joseph, assist me in my last agony. Jesus, Mary, and Joseph, may I die in peace with you. Amen.

Day 35: Meditations

1. Keep in Mind Christ Crucified

1. Keep in mind Christ crucified, and never forget his sufferings on the cross. This is the mirror with which we should look into our heart and the source from which we should draw our interior and exterior strength. The mere memory and contemplation of the mysteries of the Passion and Death of Christ afford us strength in our spiritual battles and protection from evil. Those who thankfully remember the Passion and Death of Christ are strengthened and fortified against the enemies of Christ. Therefore, be thankful to Christ for all that he has accomplished for our salvation, accept the cross he imposes upon us, and bear it after

Christ. Thus, shall we walk on the direct path that leads to heaven and gain an eternal happiness.

2. We ought to learn to forgive all who have offended us. The prayer that is offered to God in a forgiving spirit is powerful not only for our own good, but for the good of the one who has offended us. The kind Heart of Jesus is easily moved, when he sees that creatures imitate him in pardoning those who have offended them and in praying for them; in addition, we participate in the most ardent love that he manifested on the cross.

3. After his death, Jesus descended to limbo and to purgatory to free the souls therein. The Church Militant should, by prayers and suffrages, grant relief to the poor souls in purgatory, who are the Church Suffering, so that they are freed from purgatory and admitted into the kingdom of heaven. The soul that is freed from the pains of purgatory and admitted into the company of the Church Triumphant will in turn pray for the person who quickened the release of that soul from purgatory; the redeemed soul will also in turn assist that person at the hour of that person's death to inherit eternal life.

2. Act of Praise to the Blessed Virgin Mary

O Mary, Virgin Mother of God, Martyr of love and sorrow, I praise you for having witnessed the pains and torments of Jesus, for having cooperated in the great work of my redemption, for having suffered innumerable afflictions in union with those of your Son, Jesus Christ, and for having offered to the Eternal Father all your sufferings and sorrows in union with the sacrifice of Jesus Christ on the cross for the salvation of souls. And I thank you for your maternal love to me. O Most Sacred Virgin, may my praise be accepted by you; grant me strength against your enemies. Intercede for me before your Son, and obtain for me the pardon for my sins, the remedy for all my spiritual illnesses, and the salvation of my soul. May your intercession, which is never unanswered before God, help me steadily to crucify my disordered passions to the cross of Christ and to attain the perfect amendment of my life. And persevering in divine grace until death, may I obtain eternal life through the merits of the Passion and Death of Jesus Christ our Lord. Amen.

V. Sorrowful and Immaculate Heart of Mary.

R. Pray for us who have recourse to you.

Let us pray. O Most Sacred Lamb of God, with gratitude to the Three Persons of the One Adorable Trinity, I give you thanks for all the dread anguish you endured when you were so pitilessly fastened to the cross with iron nails driven through your Sacred Hands and Feet; so that your Sacred Heart shuddered and your whole frame quivered with agony. By this your strong pain and your most bitter death and by the intercession of the Blessed Virgin Mary, I beseech you to wash away all the sins of my hands and my feet, to turn away our Father's wrath from me by showing him for me your most sacred Wounds and precious Blood, and to grant me, one day, the joys of eternal life. You live and reign with the Father and the Holy Spirit, one God, forever and ever. Amen.

WEEK 6: THE SIXTH SORROW OF THE BLESSED VIRGIN MARY - THE TAKING DOWN OF THE BODY OF JESUS FROM THE CROSS

When they came to Jesus and saw that he was already dead, they did not break his legs, but one of the soldiers thrust his lance into his side, and immediately flowed out blood and water. After this, Joseph of Arimathea, secretly a disciple of Jesus for fear of the authorities, asked Pilate if he could remove the body of Jesus. And Pilate permitted it. So he came and took his body. Nicodemus, the one who had first come to him at night, also came bringing a mixture of myrrh and aloes weighing about one hundred pounds. They took the body of Jesus and bound it with burial cloths along with the spices, according to the Jewish burial custom. (Jn. 19:33-35, 38-40).

Day 36:   The Piercing of the Side of Jesus

1. The Piercing of the Side of Jesus by Longinus

After the death of Jesus, Mary, the Mother of Jesus, continued standing near the cross. With her was Mary Cleophas, Mary Magdalen, and John, the beloved disciple. She was now concerned with the burial of Jesus and who would help her take down the body of Jesus from the cross. Inundated with this sorrowful anxiety, she turned to her

181

body guards of angels and spoke to them, saying: Ministers of the Most High, my friends in tribulation, you know that there is no sorrow like unto my sorrow; tell me then, how shall I take down from the cross my Son whom my soul loves; how and where shall I give him honorable burial, since this duty pertains to me as his Mother? Tell me what to do, and assist me on this occasion by your diligence.

The holy angels answered her, saying: O Queen, let your afflicted heart be prepared for what is still to come. The Omnipotent Lord Jesus has concealed his glory and power from people in order to subject himself to the cruelty of man's impious malice and has always permitted the laws established for the course of human events to be fulfilled. We are ready and able to obey you and to defend our true God and Creator; however, his will restrains us because he wishes to justify his cause to the end and to shed the rest of the blood still in him, to the last drop, for the salvation of the human race and in order that he may bind them still more firmly to make a return for his copious and redeeming love. If people do not avail themselves of this blessing as they ought, it is their fault. This answer of the angels increased the sorrow and anxiety of the afflicted Mother; for it had not yet been revealed to her that the sacred Body of her Son would be wounded by the lance. Therefore, the fear of what would happen to his sacred

Body renewed and increased her tribulation and anxiety.

At that moment an armed band of soldiers arrived at Calvary with orders from Pilate to break the bones of Jesus and the two thieves so as to hasten their death. It was the evening of the Sabbath, and in order to celebrate it with unburdened minds, the high priests had asked Pilate for permission to shatter the limbs of the three men sentenced to death so that, their death having been hastened, their bodies might be taken down from the crosses and not left on them until the following day. When they saw that the two thieves were still alive, they broke their limbs so as to hasten their death (Jn. 19:31). But when they came to Jesus and saw that he was already dead, they did not break his bones, thus fulfilling the prophecy in Exodus (Ex. 12:46), which commanded that no bones be broken in the Passover Lamb. But a soldier, by the name of Longinus, approached the cross of Christ and thrust his lance through the right side of Jesus, which pierced the Sacred Heart of Jesus from one side of the Heart to the other side of the Heart such that the point of the lance of Longinus came out on the left side of Jesus. Immediately there flowed out blood and water from the wound, as John, who saw it and who gives testimony of the truth, assures us. (Jn. 19:34).

Although, the wounding of the lance could not be felt by the body of Jesus, it was felt, nonethe-

183

less, by Mary in his stead and as if her heart had been pierced. Her own pain was further increased and exceeded by no other person's own in seeing the cruel mutilation of the Heart of her dead Son. Moved by compassion and love for Longinus and forgetful of her sorrow, she said to him: May the Almighty God look upon you with eyes of mercy for the pain you have caused to my soul!

Moved by the prayer of the Blessed Virgin Mary, God ordained that some of the blood and water from the sacred Side of Jesus should drop upon the face of Longinus and restore to him his eyesight, for he had a bad eye-sight and was almost blind in one of his eyes. At the same time that physical sight was given to his physical eyes, spiritual sight was also given to his spiritual eyes, his soul, so that he recognized immediately that the Crucified One whom he had so inhumanly mutilated is his Savior and God. Through this divine enlightenment Longinus was immediately converted. He wept over his sins and, having been cured, healed, washed clean, and saved with the blood and water which poured forth from the Sacred Heart of Jesus, Longinus openly acknowledged and confessed to the people that Christ is the true God and Savior of the world. He also begged the Blessed Virgin Mary for forgiveness, and Mary assured him that she has already forgiven him.

2. Act of Reparation to the Mother of Sorrows

O Blessed Mother of Sorrows, I cannot worthily express all my affections at the greatness of your grief and sorrows on account of the conflict between the love of a true Mother, by which you naturally desired to protect your Son, Jesus Christ, from the terrible torments and the cruelty of his enemies and, at the same time, to conform your will to that of the Most Holy Trinity. Thus, your heart was pierced by the sword of sorrow, prophesied by Simeon. Your heart was also pierced with a sword of sorrow when, in fulfillment of the prophecy of Simeon, a soldier thrust his sword through the side of Jesus, your Divine Son. When the sword pierced the flesh of your Son, it also pierced through your Immaculate Heart. Although the piercing of the lance into the side of Jesus Christ our Lord could not be felt by his sacred body, it, nonetheless, pierced your heart.

O Sorrowful Mother, the thrust of the lance into the Sacred Heart of Jesus, your Divine Son, was felt by your most blessed body in his stead and in your Immaculate Heart. Thus, a sword of sorrow cut through your heart, and we rightly call you more than martyr, since the effect of compassion in you went beyond the endurance of physical suffering. Moved by compassion and love and forgetful of your sorrow, you said to Longinus: May the

185

Almighty God look upon you with eyes of mercy for the pain you have caused to my soul!

O Virgin Mother, the lance-thrust which the Blessed Lord received in his sacred Side was cruel and very painful only to you; but its spiritual effects are beneficial to the souls of those who know of your goodness and most tenderly sweetness and love. Although it caused a great affliction to you, nonetheless, its mysterious favor brings a great relief and consolation to people in their sorrows who have recourse to you. O Mother of Sorrows, whose child I am and wish to be for all eternity, accept this humble prayer of consolation! Grant that, in imitation of you and your Son, our Lord Jesus Christ, I may learn to forgive injuries to all who offend me so that I may obtain efficacious graces from the Almighty God. And in the spirit of your Son and you, I forgive all who have ever in any way offended me not only for my good, but also for their good. May this doctrine of the pardoning of injuries remain in my heart. Be with me in my afflictions and pains, and grant me the dew of your sweet love and consolation. Come to my assistance and encourage me whenever I am assailed, console me by the sweetness of your words, and enrich me by all the blessings that flow from you who are the storehouse of all the gifts of the Holy Spirit. Obtain favors and blessings for me. Grant me your protection now and always, especially at the hour of death so that I may receive the mercies of the Lord and be granted admittance into the kingdom of heaven. Through Jesus Christ our Lord. Amen.

V. Mother of Sorrows and Mother of merciful bounty, who stood at the foot of the cross.

R. Pray for us, that we may be made worthy of the promises of Christ.

Let us pray. O Jesus, true and fruitful Vine, I thank you for shedding your most precious Blood for me and other sinners when you gave us water and blood from your pierced side, so that not one drop remained in your Heart. Then you were nailed and hung on the cross, and your tender Flesh grew pale, and your moisture was all dried up within you, and the marrow of your bones consumed. By this your most bitter Passion, by the shedding of your most precious Blood, and by the intercession of the most Blessed Virgin Mary, I beseech you, O Most Loving Jesus, wash my soul at the hour of my death with the Water which flowed from your Sacred Side, and adorn it with all the sanctity in the Precious Blood of your sweetest Heart, and render it acceptable in your sight in the fragrance of your divine and heavenly love. Amen.

Day 37: The Prayer of Mary for Divine Help Regarding the Burial Arrangements for Jesus

1. The Blessed Virgin Mary Asks God for Help Regarding the Burial of Jesus

The evening of the Passover was fast approaching, and the Blessed Virgin Mary had as yet no solution on how to go about the burial of her dead Son. However, the Lord Jesus had divinely ordained that Joseph of Arimathea and Nicodemus should relieve his Mother of the burden of laying his body to rest. They were both just men and disciples of the Lord; however, they had not as yet openly confessed themselves as disciples of the Lord for fear of the authorities, who persecuted and regarded as enemies all those who followed Christ and acknowledged him as the Messiah. The dispositions of Divine Providence concerning the burial of Jesus had not been revealed to the Virgin Mary. Thus, as evening was fast approaching, which would usher in the commencement of the Sabbath, so also was her anxiety increasing regarding how she would take down the body of Jesus from the cross and how and where she would give him a decent burial. In her affliction she raised her eyes to heaven and prayed, saying: Eternal Father and my Lord, by the condescension of your goodness and infinite wisdom I have been raised to the exalted dignity of being the Mother of your Son; and by that same bounty of an immense God you have permitted me to nurse him at my breast, to nourish him, and to accompany him to his death. Now it behooves me as his Mother to give honorable burial to his sacred Body, but I am unable to fulfill my wishes. I beseech your Divine Majesty to provide some way for accomplishing my desires. Amen.

No sooner had she finished saying the above mentioned prayer than she saw a group of men coming toward Calvary with ladders and other apparatus for the purpose of taking down the Body of Jesus from the cross. These men were Joseph of Arimathea and Nicodemus with some of their servants. Setting aside all fear of the reprisals of the authorities and caring nothing for the power of the Romans, Joseph had gone boldly to Pilate and asked for the Body of Jesus (Mk. 15:43), in order to take the Body down from the cross and to give him a decent burial. He maintained that Jesus was innocent and was the true Son of God, as witnessed by his miracles, life, and death.

2. Act of Consolation and Compassion to the Mother of Sorrows

O Blessed Virgin Mary, Beloved Mother of God, Mother of sorrows, Mother most tender, and Mother most loving, I offer you the Heart of Jesus, which abounds in all beatitude. I offer you all the Divine affections by which he predestinated, cre-

ated, and sanctified you from all eternity to be his
Mother with the same love and tenderness which
he manifested to you on earth, when you carried
him in your bosom and nourished him with your
most holy milk, and with the same fidelity with
which he obeyed you, as a Son to a Mother. I offer
you the glory and honor to which he elevated you
on the day of your Assumption into heaven, when
you were exalted above all the choirs of angels
and the saints, and proclaimed Queen of heaven
and earth. I offer you all these tokens of his love,
as if he has presented them to you anew so that
you may overlook my malice and negligence and
assist me, with all the tenderness of a Mother, now
and at the hour of my death. Amen.

V. Holy, holy, holy are you, Lord God Almighty.

R. Just and powerful are you, Lord our God,
who lives in the highest heavens and looks upon
the lowly of the earth.

Let us pray. O Lord Jesus, full of compassion, I
commend to you my spirit and my soul in union
with that love with which you commended your
own to the Father on the cross; and I place them in
the most sacred wound of your Sacred Heart, that
they may be therein protected from all the snares
of the enemy. You know, O good Jesus, and I
know by my own sad experience, how weak and
frail I am, so that I could not of myself persevere
in good, or resist temptation even for one single

hour without your assistance. Wherefore, I pray you, by the reverence due to that union wherein your humanity is united to the adorable Trinity and by that love with which the Blessed Virgin Mary is inseparably united with you, that you would unite my will to yours, and so strengthen and secure it, that it may be unable to sin against you. In union with your most sinless limbs, I commend to you all the members of my body, with all their movements, that they may move for your glory alone and for your praise and love now and forever. Amen.

Day 38: The Consolation of Mary by Joseph and Nicodemus

1. Joseph of Arimathea and Nicodemus Console Mary

Joseph of Arimathea and Nicodemus approached Mary who, in the company of John and the other holy women, stood in unconceivable sorrow at the foot of the cross. The sight of the disfigured and crucified Jesus filled Joseph and Nicodemus with deep sorrows and heart-felt pains that they prostrated themselves at the feet of Mary for a considerable length of time without speaking a word. They all wept and sighed most bitterly until Mary raised them up from the ground and consoled them. Thereupon they then saluted and consoled her.

Mary thanked them kindly for their words of consolation and for the service they were about to render to their God and Savior. She promised them eternal reward in the name of him whose Body they were to take down from the cross and afterwards lay in the tomb. Joseph of Arimathea answered: Even now, O Lady, we feel in the secret of our hearts the sweet delight of the Holy Spirit, who has moved us to such love, that we never can succeed in explaining it.

Joseph of Arimathea and Nicodemus then took off their mantles and with their own hands placed the ladders against the holy cross. They then climbed it in order to remove the sacred Body of Jesus from the cross, while his Mother stood closely by calmly, reverently, and patiently.

2. Intercessory Prayers to the Mother of Sorrows for the Souls in Purgatory

1. To you, most holy Virgin Mary, my Mother, do I turn in humble supplication, confidently praying to you, and entreating you, that, for that sword which pierced your heart, when you saw your beloved Son Jesus bow his Head and give up the spirit, you would succor the poor souls in purgatory, especially those who are dear to me. Intercede in their behalf, and show to them your blessed Son, O merciful, O kind, O sweet Virgin Mary. O Mother of Sorrows, O Queen of martyrs, for the love of Jesus, who died for us on the cross,

help us also with your powerful prayers and save our souls. O Mary, our dear Mother of grace, Mother of mercy, take pity upon us now and at the hour of our death. Amen.

2. O most sorrowful Mother, Mary, I humbly beseech you to offer up, with the bitter passion of your most beloved Son, the sighs and tears and all your grief in his sufferings to the Eternal Father so that, through the merits of them all, the souls of my relations who are now suffering in the burning flames of purgatory may obtain relief and re-freshment, and thus, freed from their pains of purgation, they may be clothed with glory in heaven, and there to praise the mercy of God for-ever and ever. Amen.

3. O Blessed Virgin Mary, we beseech you for the souls in purgatory so that through your inter-cession they may be freed from their pains of pur-gation and be granted eternal life with your Son and our Lord. By your special powers and privi-leges before the Throne of the Most Blessed Trinity and by the merits of the precious Blood of Jesus Christ, may the Most Merciful and Compassionate Father, who is worthy of all reverence and praise, bend his clemency toward them, forgive them their sins and grant them his divine pardon and presence. Amen.

V. Eternal rest grant to them, O Lord.

R. And let perpetual light shine upon them.

Let us pray. O God, Creator and Father of all the faithful, give to the souls of your departed servants the remission of all their sins so that, through the intercessions of the Blessed Virgin Mary, they may obtain the pardon which they desire and enjoy the happiness of light eternal. Grant this through our Lord Jesus Christ, your Son, who lives and reigns with you and the Holy Spirit, one God, forever and ever. Amen.

Day 39: The Taking Down of the Body of Jesus from the Cross

1. Jesus is Taken Down from the Cross

The Lord had inspired Joseph of Arimathea and Nicodemus, two members of the Pharisee class who were also secret disciples of Jesus, with the thought of caring for his burial. Thus, Joseph of Arimathea went to Pilate and asked if he could remove the Body of Jesus. And Pilate gave him permission. (Mt. 27:58). With this permission Joseph left the house of Pilate and, on his way to Calvary, he called upon Nicodemus. Joseph provided the winding sheets and burial cloths with which to wrap the Body of Jesus (Mt. 27:59). Nicodemus, who had at first come to Jesus by night, also came, bringing a mixture of myrrh and aloes, weighing about a hundred pounds. (Jn. 19:39). With these and other necessities, they made their way to Calvary. They were accompanied by their servants and some other pious and devout persons, in whom likewise the precious Blood shed for everyone by the crucified God, had begun to produce its salutary effects.

When they arrived at the foot of the cross, they paid homage to Mary, the Mother of Jesus, and she thanked them kindly, especially for the service they were about to render to their God and Savior. She promised them the eternal reward in the name of Jesus whose body they were to take down from the cross and bury in the tomb. They acknowledged the efficacy of her prayers for them and the sweet consolations they have received from the Holy Spirit for the task they are about to perform for her and her Son. Joseph of Arimathea and Nicodemus then divested themselves of their mantles and with their own hands they placed the ladders to the holy cross. They climbed up the ladders in order to detach the nails from the hands and feet of the dead Jesus on the cross and then take down the sacred Body of Jesus. The glorious Mother of Jesus stood closely by watching with equanimity and calmness.

When they had climbed up the ladder, they detached the crown of thorns from the sacred Head of Jesus, which lay bare the lacerations and deep wounds it had caused in his sacred Head. They then handed down the crown of thorns with great reverence and amid abundant tears to the Mother of Jesus. She received it on her knees, and in deepest adoration bathed it with her tears, permitting the sharp thorns to pierce her face by pressing it to her face. She asked the Eternal Father to inspire due veneration toward the sacred crown of thorns in those Christians who would obtain possession of them in future times. In imitation of the Mother of God, John and the pious women and the other faithful who were present there, also adored it. Joseph and Nicodemus also did the same with the nails, handing them first to most holy Mary for veneration and afterward, John and the pious faithful present also showed their own reverence. Thus, began the practice or devotion of placing and venerating a crown of thorns and three nails in front of churches during Lent.

Then Our Lady sat down on a bare rock and held the burial cloth that Joseph had brought with outstretched arms ready to receive the dead Body of her Son, Jesus. In order to assist Joseph and Nicodemus who have removed the nails from his hands and feet, Mary Magdalen then held the sacred Legs of Jesus while Joseph and Nicodemus gradually lowered the rest of the Body down until John could hold in his hands the sacred Head and the Back of Jesus. And then Mary Magdalen and John, with tears and reverence, placed the dead Body of Jesus into the arms of his Mother. This was to her an admixture of sorrow and consolation: for, on the one hand, in seeing him thus wounded and all his beauty disfigured beyond all the children of men (Ps. 44:3), the sorrows of her most chaste heart were again renewed; and, on the other hand, she was consoled that all his physical sufferings and pains were over and that in holding him in her arms she had taken possession of the Body of her Son. She looked upon him with supreme adoration and reverence, shedding tears profusely. The Blessed Mother held the dead Body of Jesus in her arms in order that the other people present might pay their respect to him. In union with her, as he rested on her arms, all the multitude of the angels worshipped him, although unseen by all others except Mary. After they had paid their homage and last respects, the most prudent Mother held the dead Body of Jesus for some time until Joseph of Arimathea, Nicodemus, and John besought her to allow the burial of her Son to proceed, to which she readily agreed.

2. Special Intention Prayer to the Mother of Sorrows

1. O Mother of the Lord Jesus Christ, you have the compassion of a most loving Mother. By the virtues of the great troubles that your soul suffered in the ocean of suffering and the tears you shed in the terrible sorrowful mysteries, I humbly beseech your Son, our Lord Jesus Christ, through your intercessions, to grant me the forgiveness of my sins, the grace of sincere repentance and true conversion, and the strength and perseverance to

remain faithful to him. Should I perchance soil the beauty of my soul with the least imperfection, help me rise from it at once, acknowledge it before the Most High God, and, through your intercession, receive pardon for my sins and special favors from the Most High God. Amen.

2. O ever-Virgin Mary, who was conceived without sin and who directed every movement of your pure heart to God, intercede for me who invoke you and obtain for me special graces and favors. I place under your powerful intercession the following intentions of mine. (*state your special intentions here*). O most pure and ever-blessed, only and incomparable Virgin Mary, beloved Daughter of God the Father, beloved Mother of God the Son, and beloved Dwelling-Temple of God the Holy Spirit; look down upon me with your eyes of pity and hear my supplications, O my Most Blessed Mother, help and succor me, in all things, now, always, and at the hour of my death. Amen.

V. Pray for us, O most sorrowful Virgin.

R. That we may be made worthy of the promises of Christ.

Let us pray. O Most Loving Lord Jesus, I thank you with humble and loving affection for all the blessings that I have received in abundance from you. The memory of your blessings is stored in me, and especially memorable to me are that you have entrusted me to the care and solicitude of your Blessed Mother, that you have redeemed me from the kingdom of darkness and transferred me to your Kingdom, which is a Kingdom of light, life, and love and of justice, peace, and joy in the Holy Spirit. I also thank you that you have called me to follow you, that you have drawn me closer to you, that you have dissembled and excused my sins and faults, and that you have added thereto many favors to me. O Lord Jesus, I thank you for all the blessings which you have wrought for me and for the whole human race. Amen.

Day 40: The Descent of Jesus into Limbo and Purgatory

1. Jesus Frees the Souls in Limbo and in Purgatory

Later that same evening of Good Friday when she was alone in the Cenacle, Mary, in a vision, saw the doings of the most holy Soul of her Son after it left his sacred Body. The Blessed Mother saw the Soul of Christ, which remained united to his Divinity, descend to limbo to release the souls imprisoned therein. They could neither enter heaven nor enjoy the vision of God until the Redemption of the human race was accomplished by Christ and until Christ should open the gates of heaven closed by the sin of Adam.

She saw the most holy Soul of Christ Jesus our Lord go into limbo in the company of innumerable angels, who gave glory, praise, and worship to the victorious and triumphant King. In accordance with his greatness and majesty, the holy angels commanded the portals of the ancient prison of limbo to open in order that the King of glory, who is powerful in battle and who is the Lord of virtues, might find the gates unlocked and opened at his entrance. Upon entering into limbo, the souls therein worshipped him, and gave him thanks and glory, breaking forth in the canticle of praise of the holy angels. They sang saying: The Lamb that was slain is worthy to receive power and divinity, and wisdom, and strength, and honor, and glory and benediction. You have redeemed us, Lord, by your blood, out of every tribe, and tongue, and people, and nation and you have made us to our God a kingdom and priests, and we shall reign on the earth. (Rev. 5:12). Yours, O Lord, is the power, yours the reign, and yours is the glory of your works. The Lord then commanded the angels to release all the souls in limbo.

After the souls have been released from limbo, Jesus and the angels went with them to meet the souls in purgatory, where the souls of the just are purged of their sins by the fires of purgatory and their sinful deeds are fully blotted out (II Mac. 12:42) if they have not paid fully for their sins and iniquities in this life. For no one who is defiled shall enter into heaven. (Rev. 21:27). And immediately Christ gave the command for the release of all the souls in purgatory; the angels then proceeded and freed all of them at once. Christ absolved them there and then from the remainder of their punishments. And they too glorified Christ the Redeemer and joined the other souls of the just. Thus on that day the prison-houses of both limbo and purgatory were entirely emptied of all souls by the King of kings and Lord of lords.

St. Paul tells us that Jesus descended into the lower regions of the earth and that the one who descended is also the one who ascended far above all the heavens, that he might fulfill all things.[10]

Mary, seeing the souls of the just released from limbo and from purgatory, composed songs of praise to God and magnified the mysteries of his triumph and of the most loving and wise providence of the Redeemer, the omnipotent King and affectionate Lord. For he has taken possession of his reign, which was bestowed on him by the Father who has rescued his children in order that they might commence immediately to enjoy the eternal reward merited for them. She also rejoiced and gave thanks to the Lord God Almighty, who is, and who was, and who is to come, for he has taken his great power and begun to reign and for rewarding his servants, the prophets, and the saints and all who fear his name, both small and great.[11] She rejoiced and glorified the Lord as his handmaid and as his Mother.

---

[10] Eph. 4:9-10.
[11] Rev. 11:17-18.

2. Act of Commemoration of the Seven Sorrows of the Blessed Virgin Mary

1. O Blessed Virgin Mary and Mother of Sorrows, by the virtues of the sorrows that pierced your Sorrowful and Immaculate Heart at the prophecy of Simeon and by your powerful intercessions, graces, prerogatives, and privileges, grant peace to my family. Amen.
Say 1 Hail Mary.

2. O Blessed Virgin Mary and Mother of Sorrows, by the virtues of the sorrows that pierced your Sorrowful and Immaculate Heart at your flight with the Infant Jesus and with St. Joseph to Egypt and by your powerful intercessions, graces, prerogatives, and privileges, grant me enlightenment about divine mysteries. Amen.
Say 1 Hail Mary.

3. O Blessed Virgin Mary and Mother of Sorrows, by the virtues of the sorrows that pierced your Sorrowful and Immaculate Heart at the loss of the Child Jesus for three days and by your powerful intercessions, graces, prerogatives, and privileges, grant me consolation in my pains and be with me in my work. Amen.
Say 1 Hail Mary.

4. O Blessed Virgin Mary and Mother of Sorrows, by the virtues of the sorrows that pierced

your Sorrowful and Immaculate Heart at the pitiful sight of your most holy and innocent Jesus and
by your powerful intercessions, graces, prerogatives, and privileges, grant me the sanctification of
my soul and holy obedience to the will of God.
Amen.
Say 1 Hail Mary.

5. O Blessed Virgin Mary and Mother of Sorrows, by the virtues of the sorrows that pierced
your Sorrowful and Immaculate Heart at the crucifixion and death of Jesus and by your powerful
intercessions, graces, prerogatives, and privileges,
grant me your strength and protection in my spiritual battles with the infernal enemy and defend
me at every moment of my life. Amen.
Say 1 Hail Mary.

6. O Blessed Virgin Mary and Mother of Sorrows, by the virtues of the sorrows that pierced
your Sorrowful and Immaculate Heart at the
piercing of the sacred Side of Jesus with a lance
and the taking down of his sacred Body from the
cross and by your powerful intercessions, graces,
prerogatives, and privileges, grant me the grace of
a holy life and of a holy death. Amen.
Say 1 Hail Mary.

7. O Blessed Virgin Mary and Mother of Sorrows, by the virtues of the sorrows that pierced
your Sorrowful and Immaculate Heart at the buri-

al of Jesus and by your powerful intercessions, graces, prerogatives, powers, and privileges, grant me the favor of beholding your most resplendent and beautiful face as my dear Mother for all eternity. Amen.

Say 1 Hail Mary.

O Beloved Mother of Sorrows, I devoutly invoke you to obtain for me true repentance of my sins. I invoke you as my divine Mother for your strength and protection in my tribulations and that you would strengthen and protect me especially at the hour of my death. Ask your beloved Son, our Lord Jesus Christ to impress upon my heart, mind, and soul the remembrance of his Passion and to grant me his reward in heaven. I commit myself to you to dispose of me in whatever manner it might please you and to obtain for me all the graces that you desire of me. Amen.

O Mary most holy, Mother of Sorrows, by that intense martyrdom which you suffered at the foot of the cross during the three hours of the agony of Jesus, deign to aid us, children of your sorrows, in our last agony so that, by your prayers, we may pass from our death-bed to adorn your crown in the holy joys of heaven. Amen.

Mother of mercy, Mother of grace, Mary, help a fallen race. Shield us when the foe is nigh, and receive us when we die. Amen.

V. From sudden and unprepared death.

R. Deliver us, O Lord.

V. From the snares of the devil.

R. Deliver us, O Lord.

V. From everlasting death.

R. Deliver us, O Lord.

Let us pray: O God, who for the salvation of the human race has made for us in the most bitter death of your Son both an example and a protection for us; grant, we beseech you, that we may be found worthy to obtain the full effect of his great love now and at the hour of death, and to be made partakers of the glory of our Redeemer. Through the same Christ our Lord. Amen.

Day 41: The Power of Jesus and Mary over the Powers of Hell

1. The Names of Jesus and Mary are Feared in Hell

When Christ descended to the land of the dead to free the souls in limbo and those in purgatory, the apostate angels and the damned in hell, by the disposition of the Most High, were made to see and feel the descent of the Redeemer into limbo and purgatory. The demons were filled with utter confusion and grave torments by the utmost, crushing defeat they had suffered at the hand of Christ on Mount Calvary. When they heard the voices of the good angels advancing with the King of kings into limbo, the bad angels were confounded and terrified anew. Like serpents pursued, they hid themselves and clung to the hottest and most remote pits of hell. The souls of the damned regretted more intensely their hellish pains and their loss of eternal salvation.

In addition, the demons and the damned acknowledged the Divinity of the Christ and the redemption he has wrought for the human race by his sufferings and by his death on the cross. They also acknowledged the mighty and invincible power of the Blessed Virgin Mary, the Mother of the Christ over all creation. The names of Jesus, Mary, and Joseph are feared in hell. On account of the defeats they suffered at the hand of Jesus and Mary, the infernal spirits resolved there and then to be more ferocious, cunning, and deceitful in their persecutions of Catholics, especially those who are devoted to the Blessed Virgin Mary (Rev. 12:17). Nonetheless, the holy names of Jesus and Mary are feared in hell.

At the pronouncement of the holy names of Jesus and Mary, many souls have been saved from the claws of the powers of darkness. She has often snatched souls from the claws of her enemies and has always brought such souls both terrestrial and celestial joys. God has conceded to the Blessed Virgin Mary the special privilege of securing the eternal happiness of those who are devoted to her and who should call upon her in life, and especially at the hour of death, constituting her as their Mother, Advocate, and Protectess in heaven. The inconceivable charity of the Blessed Virgin Mary toward all living souls lends her to come to the aid of those who invoke her or who invoke her on behalf of others. She is ever-ready to assist and guide everyone to eternal life. The Lord Jesus has conceded to her so many privileges as his Mother. God the Father has honored her to be the Mother of his only-begotten Son, God the Son has chosen her to be his Mother, and God the Holy Spirit has chosen her to be the Mother of all living creatures. She has so many sources of help and graces at her disposal solely for the benefit of mortals. As the Mother of clemency and love, it brings her great joy to see people call upon her for their material wellbeing and for the eternal salvation of their soul.

2. Act of Commemoration of the Joys of the Blessed Virgin Mary

1. Hail Mary, White Lily of Heaven, I rejoice with you, and I give thanks and praise to the ever-Blessed Trinity who granted you the glorious grace and privilege of your holy and Immaculate Conception.

2. Hail Mary, Mystical Rose of Heaven, I rejoice with you, and I give thanks and praise to the ever-Blessed Trinity who granted you the glorious grace and privilege of your holy Nativity.

3. Hail Mary, Priceless Pearl of Heaven, I rejoice with you, and I give thanks and praise to the ever-Blessed Trinity who granted you the glorious grace and privilege of your most holy name of Mary.

4. Hail Mary, Shining Star of Heaven, I rejoice with you, and I give thanks and praise to the ever-Blessed Trinity who granted you the glorious grace and privilege of your holy Presentation.

5. Hail Mary, Bright Moon of Heaven, I rejoice with you, and I give thanks and praise to the ever-Blessed Trinity who granted you the glorious grace and privilege of your holy Betrothal.

6. Hail Mary, Radiant Star of Heaven, I rejoice with you, and I give thanks and praise to the ever-Blessed Trinity who granted you the glorious grace and privilege of your holy Annunciation.

7. Hail Mary, Virgin Mother of Heaven, I rejoice with you, and I give thanks and praise to the ever-Blessed Trinity who granted you the glorious grace and privilege of your holy Visitation.

8. Hail Mary, Pure Joy of Heaven, I rejoice with you, and I give thanks and praise to the ever-Blessed Trinity who granted you the glorious grace and privilege of your holy Motherhood.

9. Hail Mary, Crystal Mirror of Heaven, I rejoice with you, and I give thanks and praise to the ever-Blessed Trinity who granted you the glorious grace and privilege of your holy Purification.

10. Hail Mary, Immaculate Treasure of Heaven, I rejoice with you, and I give thanks and praise to the ever-Blessed Trinity who granted you the glorious grace and privilege of your holy Assumption.

11. Hail Mary, Sacred Patroness of Heaven, I rejoice with you, and I give thanks and praise to the ever-Blessed Trinity who granted you the glorious grace and privilege of your holy Coronation.

12. Hail Mary, August Queen of Heaven, I rejoice with you, and I give thanks and praise to the ever-Blessed Trinity who granted you the glorious grace and privilege of your holy Queenship.

V. O Mary, ever-Virgin, you are clothed with the sun, with the moon beneath your feet, and on your head is a mystical crown of twelve stars.

R. O Most Sacred Virgin, may my praise be accepted by you; grant me strength against your enemies.

Let us pray. O Lord Jesus Christ, who has placed us under the patronage of your most holy Mother, come into our hearts, and pour down upon us your purifying grace, whereby we may persevere in your service, and in the service of the same most holy Virgin Mary so that fortified by so powerful a protection, we may perform those good desires which you have put into our hearts. And having accomplished all that was set before us to do, may we attain those things which you have been pleased to promise to those who abide in you. For you live and reign with the Father, in the unity of the Holy Spirit, one God, forever and ever. Amen.

Day 42:   Meditations

1.   Never Forget the Incarnation, Passion, and Death of Jesus

1.   The lance-thrust into the side of the sacred Body of Jesus was cruel and very painful to his Mother, the Blessed Virgin Mary. It caused her great affliction. She felt the pains of the lance-thrust of the sacred Side of her Son. Although she did not lose her life, nonetheless, she endured the agonies of death mysteriously. Therefore, she also experienced his resurrection in her soul. Jesus willed that his Sacred Heart, the seat of love, should be thrust with a lance so that, through this port, souls might enter therein and receive relief and so that his Sacred Heart might be a fortress for all who seek refuge therein. The mystery of the piercing of the sacred Side of Jesus also signifies that from this last pouring forth of his blood and water arose the Church, cleansed and washed by his most precious Blood. From his sacred Side, the Church has spread to the ends of the earth. The piercing of the sacred Side of Jesus also signifies his redemptive blood and the living waters that flow forth from him to every one for our salvation.

2. Consider also the ever ready providence of the Most High in coming to the aid of his children who call to him in true confidence. This was demonstrated in the case of the Blessed Virgin Mary when she found herself afflicted and at a loss concerning the proper means, ways, and place for the burial of her divine Son, Jesus. God came to her assistance in her plight by moving the hearts of Joseph and Nicodemus and of the other faithful to assist her in burying Jesus. By their opportune help in taking Jesus from the cross and in laying him to rest she was so much consoled in her tribulation. And on account of their help and her prayer the Most High filled them with wonderful graces and blessings and they were enlightened and filled with the mysteries of the Redemption. The admirable disposition of the sweet and powerful providence of God is such that in order to bless people, he sometimes allows misfortune to happen to them so as to give opportunities to other people to be charitable to those who have been afflicted with the misfortune. In this way, the beneficiary is divinely helped and the benefactor, on account of the good work he or she has done, is divinely rewarded with blessings which the benefactor would not have otherwise received.

3. A person gains merits from God each time the person performs an act of kindness even if it is no more than giving a cup of water to a disciple of Christ for the love of God. (Mt. 10:42). Thus, God

grants several blessings to a person for the performance of even the most insignificant works of charity or kindness. For example, when a person performs even the smallest act of kindness out of his or her love of God, the person expiates for his or her sins, the person receives divine strength to fight temptation, and the person advances beyond all that could offer him or her resistance in the works of God and in the performance of other good works. In addition, the soul of the person is raised to an exalted and high degree of heavenly love, the soul inches closer to the attainment of the highest and infinite Good, and the person experiences fulfillment. In addition, each time a person performs the least works of charity or acts of kindness in a state of grace the rewards due to the soul of the person in the next life increases significantly and the soul of the person in the next life would shine with great splendor.

2. Act of Praise to the Most Blessed Trinity in Honor of the Blessed Virgin Mary

Blessed be the ineffable, ever-adorable omnipotence of God the Father; and blessed the wondrous and manifold wisdom of God the Son; and blessed the most amazing and tender goodness of the Holy Spirit, the Paraclete, that the ever-glorious Trinity deigned to decree from eternity, to create in time, and to bestow on us as our most effectual help and succor, the Blessed Virgin Mary, in order that he might communicate to her his own divine and super-abounding beatitude. Amen.

V. Sorrowful and Immaculate Heart of Mary.

R. Pray for us who have recourse to you.

Let us pray. O Blessed Trinity who has neither commencement nor termination, who abounds ever in joy and beatitude, and who imparts eternal glory and blessedness to the angels and saints, I give you thanks for the Virgin Mary, the effulgent Rose of heaven, who is blessed above all creatures. I extol with the highest gratitude the incomprehensible omnipotence, inscrutable wisdom, and ineffable goodness of the Ever-Blessed Trinity forever and ever. Amen.

WEEK 7: THE SEVENTH SORROW OF THE BLESSED VIRGIN MARY - THE BURIAL OF JESUS

They took the body of Jesus, and wrapped it in linen cloths with the spices, as is the burial custom of the Jews. Now in the place where he was crucified there was a garden, and in the garden a new tomb in which no one had ever been buried. So because of the Jewish day of Preparation, as the tomb was close by, they laid Jesus there.
(John 19:40-42).

Day 43:   The Procession to the Sepulcher

1. The Procession of Angels and the Faithful to the Sepulcher

As evening was fast approaching, Joseph of Arimathea, Nicodemus, and John besought Mary, as she held the Body of her dead Son to her bosom, to permit them to proceed with the burial of Jesus, to which the most prudent Mother acquiesced. They then anointed the sacred Body of Jesus, using all the hundred pounds of the spices and the aromatic ointments brought by Nicodemus. Having anointed the sacred Body of Jesus, they then wrapped the Body from the Feet upward to the Neck with the white, linen cloths Joseph brought with him. They then used another white, linen cloth and wrapped it around the sacred Head of the dead Body of Jesus. Thus, they took the body of Jesus and wrapped it with the spices in linen cloths, according to the burial custom of the Jews. (Jn. 19:40).

It was these same cloths that John and Peter saw in the tomb after Christ had risen from the dead. For early on the first day of the week, while it was still dark, Mary Magdalene and the other Mary went to the tomb and saw that the stone had been removed from the entrance to the tomb. So the two women ran to Simon Peter and the other disciple, the one whom Jesus loved, and said to them: They have taken the Lord out of the tomb, and we do not know where they have put him. Then Peter and John ran to the tomb, but the other disciple outran Peter and reached the tomb first. When John got to the tomb, he bent down and looked inside and saw the linen wrappings lying there but he did not go in. Then Simon Peter came following him and went straight into the tomb. He saw the linen wrappings lying there, and the cloth that had been on Jesus' Head, not lying with the linen wrappings but rolled up in a place by itself. Then the other disciple, who reached the tomb first, also went in, and he saw and believed; for as yet they did not understand the scripture, that he must rise from the dead. Then the disciples returned to their homes. (Mt. 28:1, 8; Jn. 20:3-10).

In any case, when Mary, the Mother of Jesus, agreed that the burial of Jesus should proceed, she called forth from heaven many hosts of angels, together with those angels of her guard, to accompany her to the burial of Jesus. Immediately they descended from on high, which only Mary could see. And a procession of myriad of heavenly angels and of a handful of the faithful having been formed, the anointed and sacred Body of Jesus was placed on a bier by John, Joseph of Arimathea, Nicodemus, and Longinus, the soldier who had pierced the sacred Side of Jesus but who was now repentant and who had begun to confess that Jesus is Lord. The four holy men then carried the Body of Jesus on the bier and processed in sorrow to the Sepulcher. They were followed by the Blessed Mother, by Mary Magdalen, and by the rest of the women disciples. Also accompanying them were many others who had been moved by the divine light and had come to Calvary. The holy angels formed a military-style bodyguard of honor around the body of Jesus and the faithful, and they all processed to the Sepulcher.

During the procession the Sepulcher, the holy men and women, with tears, sang psalms for the dead in mournful tones. The procession from Mount Calvary to the Sepulcher took about seven minutes. Hence John says: Now in the place where he had been crucified there was a garden, and in the garden a new tomb, in which no one had yet been buried. (Jn. 19:41).

2. Act of Reparation to the Sorrowful Mother

O Blessed Virgin Mary, Mother of the Only begotten Son of God, who gave him human flesh that he might become our Brother, our Redeemer, and our Teacher, I offer myself to live and labor anew in this mortal life in his honor, according to all the decrees of his divine will and be pleasing in his sight. I also offer myself to you as your devoted child. I take you as my Most Blessed Mother and my Queen. I present myself before your immense charity and implore you from my inmost heart to turn on me those pitying eyes of yours and grant me strength and protection against the enemies of Christ. Grant that I may practice the doctrines of your Son, follow in his footsteps, obey his commandments, and grow in the fragrance of sanctity. I believe you will assist me and take care of me. Help, encourage, accompany, and preserve me in the path that leads to eternal life. Amen.

I offer my intellect and will and all the faculties of my mind to the Divine Mind to be used for the salvation of my soul and for the glory of God. I beseech you, most blessed among all creatures, to preserve, prosper, and protect me in the glory of the Lord. O purest Lady, your protection and assistance have not ever failed me in past, and neither shall they fail me now nor in the future. You have sown in my heart the fear of the Lord; guard it, cherish it, O kind and sweet Mother, that it may bring forth fruit a hundredfold and that it may not be snatched away by spiritual predators. Guide and guard me unto the end, command me as my Queen, instruct me as my Teacher, and correct me as my Mother. Let the angels and saints praise you, let all nations and generations know you; let all creatures eternally bless their Creator for you; and let my soul and all my faculties magnify you. Mother of love, of sorrow, and of mercy, pray for us now and at the hour of our death. Amen.

V. Sorrowful and Immaculate Heart of Mary.

R. Pray for us who have recourse to you.

Let us pray. O Humble and Gentle Lamb of God, who during three long hours hung so piteously upon the cross; with the affection of all your creatures, I give you thanks for that intolerable pain you endured when you were so cruelly stretched out upon your sacred cross that all your bones could be numbered. I beseech you by that pain and by the pains of your Blessed Mother, Mary ever-Virgin, to forgive me all the sins which I have ever committed against you with any member of my body. Amen.

Day 44:   The Burial of Jesus

1. Joseph of Arimathea, Nicodemus, John, and Others Assist Mary with the Burial of Jesus

The procession of the angels and the faithful stopped at the entrance of the garden of Joseph of Arimathea. The Sepulcher, which had been newly excavated, had been cleaned by the servants of Nicodemus such that the interior was neat and pleasing to the eye. When they got to the Sepulcher, the holy women proceeded to sit down in front of the Sepulcher. Hence Matthew says: Now Mary Magdalene and the other Mary were sitting there, opposite the tomb. (Mt. 27:61). However, the four men entered inside of the Sepulcher with the sacred Body of Jesus. Inside the Sepulcher, they reverently placed down the Body and anointed around the area they would lay the Body. Having completed the anointing of the inside of the Sepulcher, the men then lifted up the Body again and reverently placed it down at the burial spot. After having once more expressed their love by sorrowful tears, they came out. Then the Blessed Virgin Mary entered, knelt down close to the Head of her dead Son and wept with many tears. She then arose and neatly arranged the Body of Jesus. Then as the Queen of the Angels, she commanded some of her angels to keep guard over the sacred Body of Jesus. An angel then knelt down in prayer and adoration at the Head of Jesus and another at the Feet. It was these two angels who spoke to Mary Magdalene, Joanna, and Mary the mother of James when the women entered the tomb of Jesus on the morning of the Resurrection. The angels said to the women: You seek the living among the dead! Remember how he spoke to you, when he was yet in Galilee that he would rise on the third day. Go and tell his disciples and Peter that he goes before you into Galilee, there you shall see him. (Mk. 16:7; Lk. 24:10).

When she came out, Mary Magdalen then hastily entered, and flung some flowers, which she had gathered in the garden, on the sacred Body of Jesus. Then she clasped her hands together, and with sobs kissed the Feet of Jesus. She then returned to join the other women. Joseph of Arimathea then rolled a big stone and closed the entrance to the tomb, and they went away. Thus, Matthew says: Taking the body, Joseph wrapped it in clean linen and laid it in his new tomb that he had hewn in the rock. Then he rolled a huge stone across the entrance to the tomb and departed. (Mt. 27:59-60). And thus, Mark says: Mary Magdalene and Mary the mother of Joseph saw where he was laid. (Mk. 15:47).

2. Act of Consolation and Compassion to the Mother of Sorrows

O Mary, most holy Virgin and Queen of Martyrs, would that I could be transported to Heaven, there to contemplate the honors bestowed on you by the Most Blessed Trinity and by all the heavenly court. But since I am still a pilgrim in this valley of tears, accept my most sincere homage. In your Immaculate Heart, transfixed with so many swords of grief, I lay, once for all, my poor soul; receive me as the companion of your sorrows, and do not allow me ever to be separated from your only Son. I offer all my trials and tribulations and all my afflictions and sorrows to you in memory of the sorrows that you endured in your life on earth. May every thought of my mind and every beating of my heart, henceforth be an act of compassion for your sorrows and an act of rejoicing in the glories which you now enjoy in heaven.

Therefore, dear Mother, while I now grieve with you and rejoice to see you thus glorified, have compassion on me, and put me aright with your Son, Jesus, so that I may persevere in his friendship and good graces and so that I may be true and faithful to him. Come to my aid in all my needs and necessities. And as you once stood near your Divine Son at his death, come and assist me too on my last day in my agony and be with me so that from this cruel exile I may come to share in the glory of Heaven forever and ever. Amen.

Say 3 Hail Marys.

Let us pray. Let intercession be made for us, we beseech you, O Lord Jesus Christ, now and at the hour of our death, before the throne of your mercy, by the Blessed Virgin Mary, your Mother, whose most holy soul was pierced by a sword of sorrow in the hour of your bitter Passion. We ask this through you, Jesus Christ, Savior of the world, who lives and reigns with the Father and the Holy Spirit, one God, forever and ever. Amen.

Day 45:   The Return of Mary from the Burial of Jesus

1. The Return of Mary from the Sepulcher

After the burial of Jesus and after Joseph of Nicodemus had laid a large stone across the entrance of the Sepulcher, the holy men and women, including Mary returned in silence to Calvary. When they got back to Calvary, the Blessed Virgin Mary approached the holy cross and venerated it with deepest adoration. Thus, the Blessed Virgin Mary was the first to venerate the cross, and the tradition of the veneration of the cross on Good Friday, first began by the Mother of God, has continued till this day among the faithful. After she had venerated the cross, Joseph of Arimathea and all the rest of the mourners also emulated her by likewise venerating the cross.

It was already late and the sun had sunk when the Blessed Virgin Mary betook herself from Calvary and went in the company of the faithful to the Cenacle or upper room. When Mary and the other faithful got to the Cenacle, she retired for the night. But before retiring for the night, she thanked John, the other Marys, and the other women who had followed Christ from Galilee. She thanked them for persevering with her throughout the Passion of her beloved Son up until this time. She promised them in the name of Jesus the reward of everlasting life for following him with so much constancy and devotion. All of them with John acknowledged this great favor, and thanked the Lord for blessing them. She also thanked Joseph of Arimathea, Nicodemus, Longinus, and the others who had assisted at the burial of Jesus. They were all in tears. The most humble and prudent Lady thanked them for their service to her divine Son and the consolation they have afforded her. She then permitted them to depart. They then asked for her benediction. She imparted on them her blessings and many hidden and interior favors and graces. They asked her to get some bodily refreshment and take some rest. But she answered them saying that she shall neither rest nor be consoled until her Son and Lord had arisen from the dead. Thereupon she retired for the night.

She spent the night in sorrowful and mournful meditation on the mysteries of the Lord's Passion.

And alone in her room, she let loose with floods of tears the grief of her afflicted and bereaved soul. She recalled the frightful death of her divine Son, the mysteries of his life, his preaching and his miracles, the infinite value of the Redemption, and the new Church which he has founded and adorned with the riches of the Sacraments and the treasures of grace. However, she also meditated and rejoiced on the good fortune of the human race in having been so copiously and gloriously redeemed by the precious Blood of Jesus, and the inestimable fortune of those who would obtain eternal happiness. Mary passed the night in meditation of these high and hidden sacraments, weeping and sighing, and praising and glorifying the works of her divine Son, his Passion, his hidden judgments, the other mysteries of divine wisdom, and the unsearchable providence of the Lord.

2. Intercessory Prayer to Our Lady of Sorrows for the Conversion of Sinners

O Blessed Virgin Mary, Mother of Sorrows, we beseech you, to help us make use of our intellect and will to treat the mysteries of the Incarnation, Passion, and Death of Jesus Christ with due reverence and give the Incarnate Word the praise, worship, and adoration he duly deserves from us. Aid more souls to confess the great blessings of the Incarnation, to thank the Incarnate Word for coming to save us from the reign of darkness, and to dispose themselves for greater participation in the fruits and benefits of the Redemption wrought for us by Christ. By your intercession and by the divine light that emanate from the Eternal Divine Light himself, may more and more souls convert from their evil ways of life and may the mysteries of the Incarnate Word become more evident to them. And may they turn to Jesus with gratitude for saving them and, in turn, reform their life and live a holy and redeemed life. Amen.

O Blessed Mother of God, O most tender Mother and loving Queen, soften those hearts that are hardened so that they may be moved to tenderness at the mystery of the God-Man, Jesus Christ. I beseech the God of all consolation to grant that his Name may be sanctified, his Kingdom come, and his will be done on earth as it is in heaven; that the empire of sin may be destroyed, the Gospel may be preached to all nations, and his kingdom be established throughout all the earth; and that the Holy Name of the true and Living God may be truly honored, adored, and glorified everywhere, world without end. Amen.

V. Sorrowful and Immaculate Heart of Mary.

R. Pray for us who have recourse to you.

Let us pray. O Most Gracious Lord Jesus, mighty King, I recall to your mind with devotion and compassion all the sorrows you felt throughout your entire Body as you hung in agony on the cross, with your most Blessed Mother in agony beside you. I also recall with grief when, with your most Sacred Heart broke with excessive love and grief, you exclaimed: Father, why have you forsaken me. For all these sorrows of yours, I give you infinite thanks. Through your Sacred Heart, I offer you all your grief, pain, and torment which you endured throughout your entire lifetime on earth for all the sins of commission and omission that I have committed, for the perfect amendment of my life, and for your divine mercy upon me so that all the punishments and pains I so justly deserve by my sins may be forever wiped out and remitted. By this your anguish and dereliction on the cross, I beseech you, by the power of the Holy Spirit, to not forsake me at any time during my life-time and especially at the hour of my death. I here and now commend my spirit, soul, and body into your hand, especially at the last hour of my death so that I may die peacefully under your most loving care and protection and be admitted into the kingdom of paradise forever and ever. Amen.

Day 46: Mary at the Upper Room after the Burial of Jesus

1. Mary Asks John to Seek Out Peter and the Other Apostles

After Jesus had been laid in the Sepulcher and they had departed from the Cenacle, Joseph of Arimathea and Nicodemus, on their way back to their respective home, met Peter and the two Jameses. Joseph and Nicodemus then narrated to them the passion and death of Jesus. They all shed many tears. Peter was overwhelmed by the violent manner with which Jesus died. He embraced them, reproached himself for denying Jesus and for having been absent at the death of our Savior, and thanked them for bestowing the burial rites upon the sacred Body of Jesus.

The following morning, which was a Sabbath, the Blessed Virgin Mary asked John to meet Peter who was on the way to the city. She demanded that John should receive and console Peter kindly, and bring him to her presence. The same he was to do with the other Apostles, and that he should give them hope of her pardon and offer them her maternal love and kindness. John then proceeded from the Cenacle and shortly thereafter met Peter who was full of shame and in tears and was timidly seeking the presence of the Mother of Jesus. John consoled him and encouraged him with the message that the Mother of Jesus would like to see him. Then the two men went in search of the other Apostles. Having found some of them they together then went to the Cenacle in the hope of begging for pardon from Mary. Peter entered first and alone in the presence of the Mother of grace, he prostrated himself at her feet and, with great sorrow, said: I have sinned, O Mother of God, I have sinned before my God, and I have offended my Master and you! He could not bring himself to speak another word, for he was stifled with tearful sobs and sighs which came from the depths of his sorrowful heart.

The most prudent Virgin Mary, on the one hand, seeing that Peter has prostrated himself on the ground at her feet, considered it that he was doing penance for sins he so recently committed; however, on the other hand, she did not deem it right that Peter, the head of the Church, should prostrate himself as her feet. She then said to Peter: Arise and let us ask pardon for your guilt from my Son and our Lord. She then prayed for him, revived his hope by reminding him of the mercies of the Lord with regard to repentant sinners, and pointing out his own obligation as head of the apostolic college to give the example of constancy in the confession of the faith. By these and other arguments of great force and sweetness, she pardoned Peter, and confirmed him in the hope of pardon by the Lord.

Then the other Apostles who had deserted Jesus at the Garden of Olives, seeing that Mary, the Mother of Jesus, had forgiven Peter, summoned up courage and came forward to the Most Blessed Mary. They, too, prostrated themselves to the ground before her and asked pardon for their desertion and cowardice in forsaking her divine Son during his sufferings. They wept bitterly over their sin, being moved to greater sorrow by the presence of his Mother who was in sorrow and mourning the death of her Son. Her wonderfully sweet countenance caused in them divine graces of contrition for their sins and of greater love of Jesus. Mary raised them up and encouraged them, promising them the pardon they sought and her intercession to obtain it.

At the approach of evening she again retired, leaving the Apostles now renewed in spirit and full of the consolation and joy in the Lord, yet also full of grief for the Passion of Jesus. They were all filled with new fervor and new increase of graces.

In her retirement during the second evening following the death of Jesus, she contemplated the doings of the most holy Soul of her Son after it left the sacred Body. For the Blessed Mother knew that the Soul of Christ, united to the Divinity, descended to limbo and to purgatory to release the holy souls from those subterranean prisons, where they had been detained by the justice of God since the death of the first just man until Christ would come and release them and bring them to heaven. Mary, the Mother of Jesus, spent the rest of her earthly life helping to establish the infant Church. Thus, she is also rightly called the Mother of the Church.

2. Special Intention Prayer to the Blessed Mother of Sorrows

O Blessed Virgin Mary, you are my Advocate in the day of judgment. If on that day you most justly refuse your intercession to me, who have foolishly despised and forgotten so many and so great favors and blessings of the Lord, the results of the divine love of the Son of God and your Son, what excuse shall I have, who have been so well informed, so much admonished and enlightened by the truth? Plead my cause ever before the divine throne of mercy. O Mother of God, refresh in my memory the works of your most holy Son so that I may imitate them with all my fervor, add virtue to virtue, and seek thereby evermore to please Christ. All my merits I offer up for souls, uniting them with the merits of your dear Son in the presence of the Eternal Father and by the power of the Holy Spirit. Amen.

All generations call you blessed, and all the nations recognize and praise your grace and beauty! The earth is made illustrious by your birth. Graciously condescend toward me and bless me. I bless and magnify the Most High God for his blessings and benefits to you. By your love for the Most High console, alleviate, and enliven me, and by your natural compassion, procure for me all corporeal and spiritual blessings, especially the following special intentions. (*state your intentions here*).

Grant me also your blessing, help, and protection. May your intercession and favor never fail me. I honor and acknowledge you, O ever-Blessed Virgin Mary, as the Mother of the Incarnate Word and as my Queen and Mother who is enthroned at the right hand of your Son, Jesus Christ, our Lord forever and ever. Amen.

V. Pray for us, O most sorrowful Virgin.

R. That we may be made worthy of the promises of Christ.

Let us pray. O Most Loving Lord Jesus, I thank you with humble and loving affection for all the blessings that I have received in abundance from you. The memory of your blessings is stored in me, and especially memorable to me are that you have entrusted me to the care and solicitude of your Blessed Mother, that you have redeemed me from the kingdom of darkness and transferred me to your Kingdom, which is a Kingdom of light, life, and love and of justice, peace, and joy in the Holy Spirit. I also thank you that you have called me to follow you, that you have drawn me closer to you, that you have dissembled and excused my sins and faults, and that you have added thereto many favors to me. O Lord Jesus, I thank you for all the blessings which you have wrought for me and for the whole human race. Amen.

Day 47:   Mary at the Temple on Holy Saturday

1.   Mary Visits the Temple on Holy Saturday

The Blessed Virgin and some of the other holy women, on Holy Saturday, went to the temple. The Blessed Virgin visited the temple with the other holy women for the purpose of taking them on a holy pilgrimage of the places in the temple that were special to her. When the holy women got to the temple, they stood in silence and contemplated the damages that the earthquake of the previous day, Good Friday, had wrecked in the temple. (Mt. 27:51). The Blessed Virgin Mary then took the other holy women on a pilgrimage through all the places in the temple which were particularly special to her. She pointed out to them in the temple the spot where she was presented as a child, the spot where she was betrothed to St. Joseph, and the spot where she stood when she presented Jesus and Simeon prophesied that a sword of sorrow would pierce her heart. (Lk. 2:34-35). The remembrance of his words made her weep bitterly, for the prophecy had indeed been fulfilled, and a sword of sorrow had indeed pierced her heart. She continued with the tour and showed the women the spot where she found Jesus, on the third day when she lost him at the age of twelve, teaching the scholars of the law in the temple. At each place in the temple where Jesus had sanctified by his presence, Mary would lead the other women in respectfully kissing the ground and praying over those special places. When the holy women had finished the religious tour of the temple, they returned to the cenacle.

2. The Chaplet of Our Lady of Sorrows

The Promises of Our Lady to Those Who Honor her through her the Chaplet of our Lady of Sorrows.

1. I will grant peace to their families.
2. They will be enlightened about the divine mysteries.
3. I will console them in their pains and I will accompany them in their work.
4. I will give them as much as they ask for as long as it does not oppose the adorable will of my divine Son or the sanctification of their souls.
5. I will defend them in their spiritual battles with the infernal enemy and I will protect them at every instant of their lives.
6. I will visibly help them at the moment of their death—they will see the face of their Mother.
7. I have obtained this grace from my divine Son so that those who propagate this devotion to my tears and dolors will be taken directly from this earthly life to eternal happiness, since all their

sins will be forgiven and my Son will be their eternal consolation and joy.

The Chaplet of Our Lady of Sorrows:

Opening Prayer: O Loving Father, have mercy on me for the many sins I have committed against you. O Christ Jesus, my only Salvation and Hope, grant that all my transgressions may be blotted out by your most efficacious death. O Holy Spirit, I grieve for having sinned against you because you are so good; and with the assistance of your grace I will never sin again.

O Eternal Father, I offer, by the power of the Holy Spirit, my prayers of the Chaplet of Our Lady of Sorrows to give glory to the Most Holy Trinity, to make reparation for all the malice, negligence, and indifferences committed against the Sorrowful and Immaculate Heart of Mary, to convert sinners, to save the dying, to free the souls in purgatory, and to obtain contrition and pardon for my sins, the remission of all the punishments and pains due to my sins, the perfect amendment of my life, and all the promises and graces granted to those who honor the Blessed Virgin Mary in her sorrows. Through Christ our Lord. Amen.

Sorrowful and Immaculate Heart of Mary, pray for us who have recourse to you.

The First Sorrow of the Blessed Virgin Mary: The Prophecy of Simeon.
Say 1 Our Father, and 7 Hail Marys.

The Second Sorrow of the Blessed Virgin Mary: The Flight into Egypt.
Say 1 Our Father, and 7 Hail Marys.

The Third Sorrow of the Blessed Virgin Mary: The Loss of the Child Jesus.
Say 1 Our Father, and 7 Hail Marys.

The Fourth Sorrow of the Blessed Virgin Mary: The Meeting of Jesus and Mary When He was Carrying his Cross to Calvary.
Say 1 Our Father, and 7 Hail Marys.

The Fifth Sorrow of the Blessed Virgin Mary: The Crucifixion and Death of Our Lord Jesus Christ.
Say 1 Our Father, and 7 Hail Marys.

The Sixth Sorrow of the Blessed Virgin Mary: The Taking Down of the Body of Jesus from the Cross.
Say 1 Our Father, and 7 Hail Marys.

The Seventh Sorrow of the Blessed Virgin Mary: The Burial of Jesus.
Say 1 Our Father, and 7 Hail Marys.

On the three small beads: Pray 3 Hail Marys in honor of the tears of our Sorrowful Mother.

V. Pray for us, O most sorrowful Virgin.
R. That we may be made worthy of the promises of Christ.

Let us pray. Grant, we beseech you, O Lord Jesus Christ, that the Most Blessed Virgin Mary, your Mother, whose most holy soul was pierced by a sword of sorrow in the hour of your bitter Passion, may intercede for us before the throne of your mercy, now and at the hour of our death. Through you, Jesus Christ, Savior of the world, who lives and reigns with the Father and the Holy Spirit, one God, for ever and ever. Amen.

Day 48: Christ is Raised From the Dead

1. The Resurrection of Jesus Gives Joy and New Life to Mary

The Pharisees and Scribes, restless, confused, and disturbed by their having put Jesus to death and by the earthquake that accompanied his death, went to Pilate on the morning of the Sabbath and asked him for soldiers to guard the Sepulcher. Christ, they argued, had openly said that after three days he would rise from the dead; however, his disciples might steal the body and then say that he has risen. Pilate yielded to this malicious request and gave them the guards they desired, which they stationed at the Sepulcher (Mt. 28:12). After Christ arose from the dead, they bribed the soldiers to testify that Jesus had not arisen, but that he had been stolen by the disciples. Inasmuch as no counsel can prevail against God (Prov. 21:30), the Resurrection of Christ from the dead has become so much the more believed and confirmed.

The Resurrection of Jesus from the dead gave joy and new life not only to his own body, but also to the heart and soul of his Blessed Mother. By virtue of the Resurrection of Jesus, the sorrows of the Blessed Virgin Mary were transformed into joy, her pains into gladness, her grief into ineffable jubilation, and her sadness into elation. With acts of worship, canticles of praise, and prayers of joy, she thanked God the Father who had decreed the Resurrection of Christ from the dead, God the Son who has resurrected from the dead, and God the Holy Spirit who, by his almighty power, raised Jesus Christ from the dead. On this occasion, she received new life more abundantly (Jn. 10:10). She also received graces of celestial jubilation and joy that healed in a wonderful way the sorrows and tribulations she had undergone in the Passion of her Son, Jesus Christ. Let us celebrate the Life, Death, and Resurrection of Jesus Christ. Let us commiserate with the Mother of God, Mary ever-Virgin, for her sorrows and sufferings, and let us congratulate her for both her terrestrial and celestial joys and victories. And let us, with loving praise and gratitude, thank the Most Blessed Trinity for all graces and blessings bestowed upon the Blessed Virgin Mary and upon us.

2. Act of Commemoration of the Joys of the Blessed Virgin Mary

Hail to you, O Blessed Virgin Mary. Hail to you, O Sacred Virgin Mary. Hail to you, O Holy Virgin Mary. Blessed are you, and worthy of all praise. For you bore the Sun of Justice, Christ our Lord. You are all beautiful and there is no stain of sin in you. You are the glory of the heavenly Jerusalem. You are the honor of the people of God. You are she who magnifies his name. You are the Advocate of sinners who defends them against their proud enemy and who intercedes for them before the throne of your Divine Son! Hail Mary, full of grace and all perfection. In you is deposited the treasures and graces of the Most Blessed Trinity. Most blessed are you among all the creatures of God. Let angels and mortals praise you. Let all generations know, praise, and exult your dignity. O Blessed Mother of God and my advocate, turn on me those pitying eyes of yours. I pray, one day, to see your sight and the Most Blessed Trinity in the heavenly fatherland forever and ever. Amen.

Hail Mary, Priceless Pearl of Heaven! Hail Mary, White Lily of the glorious and ever-serene

Trinity! Hail Mary, Radiant Rose of heavenly fragrance! Of you the King of heaven was born, and by your milk he was nourished! Nourish my soul with effusions of divine grace, and uphold and succor me, a miserable sinner, now and at the hour of my death. Amen.

V. Blessed be the Holy and Immaculate Mother of God.

R. Pray for us who have recourse to you.

Let us pray. I give thanks to you, O God the Eternal Father who, in your divine omnipotence, created the Blessed Virgin Mary, exempted her from original sin, and illumined, sanctified, and blessed her to be the Mother of your only begotten Son, Jesus Christ. Let the power of your majesty and the immensity of your love for her be glorified, praised, and proclaimed for all eternity. I give thanks to you, O God the Eternal Son who, in your divine wisdom, elected the Blessed Virgin Mary to be your Mother, made her to be conceived without sin, assumed her body and soul to heaven, and elevated her as Queen of all creatures. Let all creatures in heaven, on earth, and in hell, praise and worship you on account of your love for her. I give thanks to you, O God the Holy Spirit who, in your divine goodness, gave humanity to the Incarnate Word in the womb of the Blessed Virgin Mary, descended as tongues of fire upon her and on the Apostles on Pentecost Day, and enriched her with all the favors and gifts of your powerful right hand. Let the sanctity and equity of your love for her be praised and magnified for all eternity. Through Christ our Lord. Amen.

Day 49:   Meditations

1.   The Promises of Our Lord to Those Who Honor the Sorrows of the Blessed Virgin Mary

1. Those who before death invoke the Divine Mother in the name of her sorrows will obtain true repentance of all their sins.

2. He will protect all who have this devotion in their tribulations; He will protect them especially at the hour of death.

3. He will impress upon their minds the remembrance of his Passion, and they shall be rewarded for it in heaven.

4. He will commit such devout clients to the hands of Mary, with the power to dispose of them in whatever manner she might please and to obtain for them all the graces she might desire.

2.   Act of Consecration to Mary Mother of Sorrows

Hail, O Blessed Virgin Mary, Mother of Sorrows! Hail, O Sacred Virgin Mary, Mother most loving! Hail, O Most Blessed Mary, Mother of the Crucified Christ. With devout intention, I invoke you as my Most Blessed Mother and my Advocate before your Divine Son. On the cross, your Son and our Lord, Jesus Christ, entrusted me to your maternal care and protection. I consecrate myself to you under your title and advocacy of Mary, Mother of Sorrows. I place into your hands the salvation of my soul; take charge of my salvation and lead my soul to the heavenly fatherland to praise, with you and all the angels and saints, the Most Blessed Trinity forever and ever. Amen.

O Most Chaste Virgin Mary, I beseech you by that most spotless and exceeding purity by which you prepared within your virginal womb a most sacred and sacrosanct sanctuary for your Divine Son and by your intercession that I may be cleansed from every stain of sin. O Most Humble Virgin Mary, I beseech you by that most profound humility by which you merited to be raised high above all the choirs of angels and the saints and by your intercession that all my sins may be forgiven and all the punishments and pains due thereof be expiated. O Most Loving Virgin Mary, I implore you by that ineffable love which unites you so closely and so inseparably to God and by your intercession that I may receive an abundance of all merits. Amen.

O Most Loving Mother, you received the singular honor from the ineffable kindness of the Most High God to be the Mother of his only begotten Son, Jesus Christ our Lord. I praise all the works that you performed as the Mother of his only begotten Son in having borne him and in having nourished him. Let God be eternally praised in his infinite power, wisdom, love, and goodness who formed you and who so wonderfully appointed you for our emulation in holiness and for the glory of his most holy name. Amen.

Say 3 Hail Marys.

Let us pray. O Most Loving Father, I implore you, by that surpassing love with which Jesus Christ endured all the wounds of his most holy Body and with which the Blessed Virgin Mary endured all her sorrows and sufferings in union with those of Jesus Christ our Lord, to have mercy on me and on all sinners, and on all the faithful, living and departed. Grant unto us grace and mercy, remission of sins, and everlasting life. Amen.

O Most Loving Jesus, I bless your most kingly Heart with that love with which the Holy Spirit formed you of the most chaste blood of the Virgin Mary. I offer you all the divine affections with which you predestinated, created, and sanctified her from all eternity to be your Mother. At the foot of the cross, you entrusted us to her to be our Blessed Mother. I humbly beseech you, by the love with which you love her and by the goodness which prompted you to give us so dear and so good a Mother, to hear my prayer and receive my soul into your kingdom of glory with the same affection with which you received hers when she went forth from her sacred body to you. Glory and praise to you, Lord Jesus Christ, King of endless glory, forever and ever. Amen.

O Most Loving Holy Spirit, I give thanks to you, through the bitter Passion of Jesus Christ, in union with the sorrows and sufferings of the Blessed Virgin Mary, for all your benefits to me. I offer to you the pains and tears and dolors of our Blessed Lord and of our Blessed Mother, in expiation for all the sins by which I have so often offended you. I beseech you, by the precious Blood of Jesus, to supply for all my defects and sins and to please you always. Amen.

3. Concluding Prayer

O Loving Lord Jesus, True God and True Man, have mercy on me, and deign to supply for all my defects, distractions, and negligence in my spiritual journey with the Blessed Virgin Mary, your Mother in her sorrows and joys. I offer these readings, meditations, and prayers of mine to the praise and glory of the Most Holy Trinity through your Sacred Heart so that they may be therein cleansed and perfected and so that they may be pleasing and acceptable to the Most Holy Trinity forever and ever. Amen.

68655958R00141

Made in the USA
Columbia, SC
09 August 2019